BEETHOVEN

PIANO SONATAS
Op. 31, Nos. 1, 2, 3; Op. 49, Nos. 1, 2;
Op. 53; Op. 54; Op. 57; Op. 78

EDITED BY STEWART GORDON

AN ALFRED MASTERWORK EDITION

Cover art: Ludwig van Beethoven *(1770–1827)*
by Karl Stieler (1781–1858)
Oil on canvas, 1819
Beethoven-Haus, Bonn, Germany
Erich Lessing/Art Resource, NY
Additional art: © Planet Art

Alfred

Supervising Editor: Sharon Aaronson
Music Engraving: Bruce Nelson
Cover Design: Dana D'Elia

Copyright © MMVIII by Alfred Publishing Co., Inc.
All rights reserved. Printed in USA.
ISBN-10: 0-7390-4552-0
ISBN-13: 978-0-7390-4552-7

LUDWIG VAN BEETHOVEN

Thematic Index

Piano Sonatas `VOLUME III`
Edited by Stewart Gordon

Contents

About This Edition

Ludwig van Beethoven (1770–1827) is often regarded as a link between the balance and clarity of Classicism and the emotional intensity and freedom of Romanticism. In his 32 piano sonatas, he experimented constantly with structure and content. These works span a period of almost 30 years of Beethoven's mature creative life. He used the sonatas as a workshop in which to try out innovations, many of his compositional techniques appearing in the sonatas first and then later in chamber or symphonic works.

Of the nine sonatas in this volume, autographs exist for only the Op. 53, Op. 57, and Op. 78. This edition is based on these autographs, as well as the first editions of the sonatas engraved by various contemporary publishers. In addition, a number of other esteemed editions were referenced when decisions had to be made due to lack of clarity or consistency in the early sources, or when realization of ornamentation was open to question. Editors that have been referenced are (in alphabetical order): d'Albert,[1] Arrau,[2] Bülow,[3] Casella,[4] Craxton/Tovey,[5] Hauschild,[6] Köhler/Ruthardt,[7] Krebs,[8] Martienssen,[9] Schenker,[10] Schnabel,[11] Taylor,[12] and Wallner.[13] In the context of the footnotes, the editions with more than one contributing editor are referenced in an abbreviated manner, using only the last name of either the first editor or of the more prominent editor. Recommended solutions to problems are suggested in this edition. If, however, a problem is such that it is open to several solutions, other editors' conclusions are also often included in the footnotes. In this way students and their teachers are not only offered choices in individual cases but, more importantly, gain an awareness of the editorial and performance problems that attend studying and playing this music.

The insurmountable problems that arise in trying to distinguish between the staccato dot and the wedge in these works have led this editor to join ranks with most others in using but one marking (dot) for both symbols. The reasons behind this decision and the exceptions to it are clarified in the essay on Articulation.

Like almost all other editors, I have chosen not to indicate pedaling markings in the sonatas except those left by the composer. Factors such as aesthetics of the period, Beethoven's personal sense of coloration in instruments he used, the variety of pedal mechanisms he encountered, and the subtlety of the art of pedaling in itself form a network of variables that would render traditional pedal markings of little help at best and misleading at worst. Rather, the matter of pedaling, especially as might be applicable to music of this era, must be based on innumerable choices that result from stylistic awareness and careful listening, these possibilities changing as different instruments or performance venues are encountered.

Both autographs and first editions contain inconsistencies. First editions especially are prone to many discrepancies, such as differences in articulation in parallel passages in expositions and recapitulations of movements in sonata-allegro form, or the many cases of an isolated note in passagework without the articulation shown for all its neighbors. Even those editors whose philosophy is to be as faithful to the composer as possible subscribe to the practice of correcting these small discrepancies without taking note of such through the addition of parentheses. This edition also subscribes to that practice to avoid cluttering the performer's pages with what would turn out to be a myriad of parenthetical changes. By the same token, this editor has proceeded with an attitude of caution and inquiry, so that changes have been made only in the most obvious cases of error or omission. If, in the opinion of the editor, there seemed to be the slightest chance that such inconsistencies could represent conscious variation or musical intent on the part of the composer, the issue has been highlighted, either by the use of parentheses that show editorial additions or footnotes that outline discrepancies and discuss possible musical intent on the part of the composer.

---

[1] Ludwig van Beethoven, *Sonatas for Piano*, ed. Eugen d'Albert (New York: Carl Fischer, 1981, originally published in 1902).

[2] Ludwig van Beethoven, *Sonaten für Klavier zu zwei Händen*, ed. Claudio Arrau, revised by Lothar Hoffmann-Erbrecht (Frankfurt: C. F. Peters, 1973).

[3] Ludwig van Beethoven, *Sonatas for the Piano*, ed. Hans von Bülow and Sigmund Lebert, trans. Theodore Baker (New York: G. Schirmer, 1894, currently distributed by Hal Leonard, Milwaukee).

[4] Ludwig van Beethoven, *Sonatas for Piano*, ed. Alfredo Casella (Rome: G. Ricordi, 1919).

[5] Ludwig van Beethoven, *Complete Pianoforte Sonatas*, ed. Harold Craxton, annotated Donald Francis Tovey (London: Associated Board of the Royal School of Music, 1931).

[6] Ludwig van Beethoven, *Sonaten für Klavier*, ed. Peter Hauschild (Vienna and Mainz: Wiener Urtext Edition, Schott/Universal, 1999).

[7] Ludwig van Beethoven, *Sonaten für Klavier*, ed. Louis Köhler and Adolf Ruthardt (Frankfurt: C. F. Peters, originally published in 1890).

[8] Ludwig van Beethoven, *Sonatas for Piano*, ed. Carl Krebs (Miami: Warner Bros. Publications of Kalmus Editions, originally published in 1898).

[9] Ludwig van Beethoven, *Sonaten für Klavier zu zwei Händen*, ed. Carl Adolf Martienssen (New York: C. F. Peters, 1948).

[10] Ludwig van Beethoven, *Complete Piano Sonatas*, ed. Heinrich Schenker with a new introduction by Carl Schachter (New York: Dover, 1975, originally published in 1934).

[11] Ludwig van Beethoven, *Sonatas for the Pianoforte*, ed. Artur Schnabel (New York: Simon & Schuster, 1935).

[12] Ludwig van Beethoven, *Piano Sonatas*, ed. Kendall Taylor (Melbourne: Allans Publishing PTY, Limited, 1989, currently distributed by Elkin Music International, Pompano Beach).

[13] Ludwig van Beethoven, *Klaviersonaten*, ed. B. A. Wallner, fingering by Conrad Hansen (Munich: G. Henle, 1952, 1980).

Fingering in parentheses indicates alternative fingering. When a single fingering number attends a chord or two vertical notes, the number indicates the uppermost or lowermost note. Octaves on black keys are usually fingered 1-4, but it is acknowledged that such fingering may prove too much of a stretch for some hands. Thus, (4) in parentheses indicates that players with small hands may want to substitute 1-5.

Ornaments such as trills, turns, and mordents are discussed in footnotes. When a single rapid appoggiatura or grace note is not footnoted, the performer should choose whether to execute it before the beat or on the beat. However, in some cases this editor indicates a preference for on-the-beat execution in the music by using a dotted line that connects the ornamental note with the base note with which it is to be played. Execution of Beethoven's ornaments is addressed in more detail in the essay on Ornamentation.

Portrait of the Composer (1802–1809)

This period of Beethoven's life began with a confrontation of his encroaching deafness. In April 1802, he took up residence in the small town of Heiligenstadt, just outside Vienna, with the hope of regaining his hearing and his health. Although he continued to be productive during the summer and early autumn, he was later overcome with depression and contemplated suicide. An unsent letter dated October 6, discovered after the composer's death and addressed to his brothers, is a profound expression of the composer's torment, the self-imposed social ostracism, and the inner struggle inherent in thinking about ending his life. Known as the *Heiligenstadt Testament*, this letter marked a turning point in the composer's psyche, for, after venting his feelings in this document, he summoned the strength to overcome his depression and never again succumbed to the same depth of despair.

The composer's professional life flourished during this time. Most of Beethoven's correspondence has to do with the creation and publication of a host of master works, including Symphonies Nos. 3, 4, 5, and 6; Piano Concertos Nos. 3, 4, and 5; the Violin Concerto, Op. 61; String Quartets, Opp. 59 ("Razumovsky") and 74; the Piano Trios, Op. 70; Violin Sonatas, Opp. 30 and 47 ("Kreutzer"); the oratorio *Christus am Oelberg*, Op. 85; the Mass in C, Op. 86; the Choral Fantasia, Op. 80, the first version of the opera *Fidelio*, Op. 72, as well as a great number of smaller works.

Beethoven often haggled with publishers over fees, reflecting his ongoing concern with financial security. In a letter written in September 1803 to the publisher Hoffmeister & Kühnel in Leipzig, the composer wrote, *"please remember that all my acquaintances hold appointments and know exactly what they have to live on; but Heaven help us! What appointment at the Imperial Court could be given to such a* parvum talentum com ego?*"* (Beethoven mistakenly wrote *com* instead of *quam*, the translation of the Latin being "such a meagerly talented person as myself."[14]) Although Beethoven continued to squeeze a living out of publication fees, commissions, and stipends, he constantly felt he needed more security. Thus, near the end of 1808, he was tempted to accept an offer from Napoleon Bonaparte's (1769–1821) brother Jerome (1784–1860), who had been appointed the Prince of Westphalia, to become the Kapellmeister at Kassel with an annual salary of 600 ducats.

Beethoven's admirers quickly rallied to head off a plan that would take Beethoven from Vienna. The Archduke Rudolf (1788–1831), Prince Franz Joseph von Lobkowitz (1772–1816), and Prince Ferdinand Kinsky (1781–1812) joined together to provide a lifetime annual annuity of 4,000 florins to Beethoven with the stipulation that he remain in Vienna. This amount, although seemingly more than Jerome's offer, was diminished in actual value because of inflation in Vienna. It was, however, enough to give Beethoven the security he desired, for on March 14, 1809, Beethoven wrote to Baron Ignaz von Gleichenstein (1778–1828) in Freiberg, *"You will see from the enclosed document, my dear, kind Gleichenstein, how honorable my remaining here has now become for me—Moreover, the title of Imperial Kapellmeister is to follow—Now you can help me look for a wife."*[15]

Beethoven's personal life up to this point had been plagued by frustration. Given to falling in love with women of higher social standing, he was ultimately rejected by each, often after a short romance, as they consummated unions with noblemen. Such had been the case with Countess Giulietta Guicciardi (1784–1856), to whom he dedicated the Op. 27, No. 2 piano sonata. Giulietta studied piano with the composer starting around 1801, but married Count Wenzel von Gallenberg (1783–1839) in 1803. Similarly, Beethoven first met Countess Josephine Deym (née Brunsvik) (1779–1821) in 1799 when she and her sister Therese (1775–1861) studied piano with him. Josephine had married Count Joseph Deym (1751–1804), but after her husband's death, her fondness for the composer developed into love. Beethoven wrote several love letters to her between 1805 and 1807, but in 1810 she married Baron Christoph von Stackelberg (b. 1777), presumably to give security and status to her children. She bore the Baron three more children, but he left her in 1813.

It is believed that Beethoven's request to Gleichenstein to *"help me look for a wife"* resulted in being introduced to Therese Malfatti (1792–1851) around 1810. For a time, the composer planned to marry her, but her family's objections to the union prevailed, and his proposal was rejected. Beethoven composed the popular piano piece *Für Elise* for Therese.

---

[14] *The Letters of Beethoven*, vol. I, ed. and trans. Emily Anderson (London: St. Martin's Press, 1961), p. 97.

[15] *Letters of Beethoven*, vol. I, p. 219.

Beethoven and the Piano

It was noted in Volumes I[16] and II[17] of this edition that Carl Czerny (1791–1857) reported that when he auditioned for Beethoven as a boy of 10, the composer had in his home a piano made by the Viennese piano maker Anton Walter (1752–1826). By November 1802, Beethoven noted in a letter that, *"when people began to think my relations with Walter were strained, a whole tribe of piano manufacturers have been swarming around me in their anxiety to serve me—and all for nothing. Each wants to make me a pianoforte exactly as I should like it."*[18] Later in the letter he stated that he *"shall then have the pleasure of seeing myself compelled to display my art on Jakesch's piano."*[19] One suspects sarcasm with regard to the pleasure of playing on the piano made by Viennese piano maker Matthias Jakesch (1783–ca. 1828). On November 23, 1803, in a letter to Breitkopf & Härtel, the composer apparently responded to an inquiry from the publisher by suggesting two other Viennese piano makers: *"Since you wish to have instruments from other manufacturers as well, I am suggesting to you also Herr Pohack, whose work is sound and whose prices and types of instruments are enclosed in this letter. I should also like to add Herr Moser, of whose prices and instruments will be sent to you shortly."*[20] These names are among the many piano makers in Vienna at the turn of the 19th century, and both are somewhat obscure. It is not known, for example, if either provided Beethoven with a piano or, indeed, if they were names of makers on whose pianos the composer had played at one time or another.

The most significant piano acquisition in this period of Beethoven's life was the gift from the French piano maker Sébastien Érard (1752–1831). Sébastien and his brother Jean-Baptiste (d. 1826) manufactured five-octave small pianos up until the late 1790s, at which point they opened a London workshop and began copying the larger English-style pianos. (See "Beethoven and the Piano" in Volumes I or II of this edition for a discussion of differences between the Viennese and English pianos.) The 1803 piano sent to Beethoven had a mahogany case that sat on three legs and was braced on the inside by four small iron pieces. Its stringing was tri-chord and its action was the heavier English action. The white keys were covered with ivory and the black keys with ebony. The keyboard compass was five and one-half octaves (from F to c''').

Pedals on pianos of the period were far from standard, instruments often being customized with special effects that were manipulated by either knee or foot pedals. The Érard given to Beethoven had four wooden foot pedals. From left to right, they functioned as follows:

"Lute" Pedal: Activating this pedal caused leather thongs to be inserted between the hammers and the strings.

Damper Pedal: Its effect was the same as on today's instruments.

"Dampening" Pedal: This pedal caused a cloth to be inserted between the hammers and strings.

"Keyboard Glide" Pedal: As on today's pianos, this pedal caused the keyboard to shift so that only one or two strings sounded on pianos with three strings per key, and one on pianos with two strings per key.

Notwithstanding the fact that the Érard must have been considered state of the art, the composer was not fond of it. In a letter to the Viennese piano maker Andreas Streicher (1761–1833) in November of 1810, Beethoven made reference to what was undoubtedly the Érard, stating, *"As for my French piano, which is certainly quite useless now, I still have misgivings about selling it, for it is really a souvenir such as no one here has so far honored me with…"*[21] In 1825 or 1826, Beethoven gave the Érard to his brother (Nikolaus) Johann van Beethoven (1776–1848), probably to make room for the new Graf piano the composer awaited. Johann, a pharmacist who had his own shop in Linz, later donated the piano to the Linz Museum. It is presently on loan to the Kunsthistorisches Museum in Vienna, where it is on display in the old musical instruments collection.

There is evidence, in fact, that Beethoven remained loyal to the Viennese instrument built by the Stein-Streicher family during the years in which the sonatas in this volume were written. (See Volume I of this edition for information on this family of piano builders.) A letter written to Andreas Streicher on May 6, 1810, implies that a Streicher piano had been in the composer's home for some time, for he stated, *"You have seen your instrument which I have here and you must admit that it is very worn out; and I frequently hear the same opinion expressed by other people…"*[22] In late July, Beethoven praises a Streicher piano he tried out, probably as a selection for Baron Georg Schall von Falenhorst (1761–1831), a major-general in the Imperial Army who gave musical parties in his home. The composer wrote to Streicher, *"I can't help it; the piano beside the door near your entrance is constantly ringing in my ears—I feel sure I shall be thanked for having chosen this one."*[23] Beethoven continued to

---

[16] Beethoven, *Piano Sonatas*, Vol. I (no. 16743), ed. Gordon (Van Nuys, CA: Alfred Publishing Co., 2002), pp. 6–7.

[17] Ibid., Vol. II (no. 22579, pub. 2005), pp. 6–7.

[18] *Letters of Beethoven*, vol. I, p. 82.

[19] Ibid., p. 83.

[20] Ibid., p. 101.

[21] Ibid., p. 300.

[22] Ibid., p. 271.

[23] Ibid., p. 281.

negotiate with Streicher to lease another piano for his own use, but by late fall, Beethoven had not received one, for the composer wrote complainingly, *"You promised to let me have a piano by the end of October; and now we are already half through November and as yet I haven't received one—My motto is either to play on a good instrument or not at all."* Beethoven signed the letter, *"All good wishes if you send me a p[ianoforte]; if not, then all bad wishes; your friend Beethoven."*[24] The degree to which Beethoven flattered Streicher in order to consummate the loan is impossible to know, but still, the composer's continuing association with the Stein-Streicher piano suggests that this instrument was the one that he worked with most often during this period.

Articulation, Dynamics and Accents, and Ornamentation in Beethoven's Music

Performers always seek definitive answers with regard to matters of articulation and ornamentation, for they like to feel secure in the knowledge that they are realizing the composer's intentions accurately. Unfortunately, Beethoven research has not been able to provide such answers for many textural problems, and it is very possible that solutions to the problems that attend research in this area will never be forthcoming. There are several reasons for this state of affairs.

There exist autographs of only 13 of the sonatas. One would assume that these manuscripts could provide evidence of Beethoven's intentions for the particular sonatas represented and by logically applying principles gleaned from study of these pages to other sonatas arrive at definite answers for performance problems. Unfortunately, such is not the case, for the autographs are often hastily written and extremely messy, so that some portions are virtually indecipherable and many pages seem riddled with apparent inconsistencies.

Scholars are confronted with a paradox. On one hand, Beethoven was a composer who was very particular about the details of his music, according to contemporary evidence such as personal letters, conversation books, and reminiscences of those who knew him. On the other hand, he leaves behind a legacy of manuscripts that are far from clear. This paradox has resulted in a veritable army of scholars throughout the 19th and 20th centuries attempting to unscramble the autographs and fathom the exact desires of the composer. Such research continues to this day but, notwithstanding its good intentions, answers to many questions remain elusive and, indeed, scholars have not always arrived at the same conclusions.

Similarly, research has been lavished on the first, or early, published editions of Beethoven's works. Two problems arise in examining these printed documents. First, engravers make mistakes and these editions, like all editions, are subject to error. Indeed, Beethoven complains in his letters about errors in published works; in one case, that of the Nägeli publication of the Op. 31 set of piano sonatas, the composer was so upset that he requested the edition be withdrawn. Secondly, printing technology of the time was not refined to a point that even a careful reader can be sure of all details. This is particularly true in the piano sonatas when one tries to determine exactly where slurs begin and end, or what kind of a staccato marking attends many of the notes.

Notwithstanding these difficulties, each generation of musicians continues to study these sources of this music in an attempt to glean as much guidance as possible with regard to how it should be performed. In this edition an attempt has been made not only to present the editor's solutions to specific problems as they arise, but also to indicate choices in instances where scholars have differed with one another.

Beethoven's autograph of Sonata No. 32 in C Minor, *Op. 111, second movement, measures 106–117*

---

[24] Ibid., p. 300.

Articulation

Dots and Wedges: When Beethoven proofread his copyist's work of both the Symphony No. 7, Op. 92 and the String Quartet, Op. 132, the composer indicated that he considered dots and wedges different types of accents. Thus, the composer notes, *"Where there is a dot above a note, a wedge must not be put, and vice-versa,"* and " ♩ ♩ ♩ ♩ *and* ♩ ♩ ♩ ♩ *are not identical."*[25]

Unfortunately, there is no further clarification by the composer, especially as such markings might apply to playing piano music instead of string music. The autographs, moreover, are frequently unclear in this regard, a given mark often looking like it could be either a dot or a wedge; and, when the marks are clear, they often exhibit inexplicable inconsistencies, the dots and wedges changing back and forth within the context of a single passage without apparent reason. First editions, moreover, never seem to differentiate, a dot-wedge marking that undoubtedly meant some degree of staccato appearing with many changes of shape and degrees of thickness.

As a result of this confusion, editors of Beethoven's piano music who often began their work with the hope of being able to differentiate between dots and wedges eventually come to realize that doing so means incorporating a lot of guesswork into their editions and making large numbers of changes in the name of consistency. Thus, most editors have given up making such differentiation and simply adopt one kind of marking in their editions. Consequently, only dots are to be found in the publications prepared by Arrau, Casella, Bülow, Geoffroy, Köhler, Krebs, Martienssen, Schnabel, and Wallner. This edition conforms to such a tradition. However, in those sonatas where the autograph is extant and examination of dots and wedges in given passages reveals enough clarity and logic to warrant consideration by performers, such information will be footnoted. Of the well-known 20th-century editors, only Schenker and Tovey attempt to use two types of accent, these editors of necessity relying on personal choice for a multitude of questionable cases.

Phrasing and/or Slurring: The aforementioned difficulties in deciphering Beethoven's autographs, as well as the vagaries and inconsistencies found in first editions, result in many problematic areas regarding phrasing or slurring. Every editor must face many instances in which the choice is to leave unaltered seemingly inconsistent phrasing or to "correct" such cases by applying generally accepted musical principles and/or logic. Some editors are quick to assume error and make changes. Others are more apt to leave the original in place, adopting as much clarity as possible, and let the performer decide at some point in time whether or not the inconsistency is part of the composer's intent. In this edition, the textual source has been preserved in a high percentage of these cases. Frequently the inconsistency has been pointed out to highlight the problem for the performer, particularly in those cases where well-known 20th-century editors seem to have differed markedly with each other or are at odds with the source of the text.

In addition to the difficulty of clarity and consistency, there is a problem that is part of a larger performance practice issue attending much of he music of the late-18th and early-19th centuries. It can be observed that much of this music comes to us by way of autographs or first editions with phrasing or slurring patterns that frequently stop at points that rob the phrase of a long-line concept. These points often fall at the ends of measures.

Late-19th-century musical thinking emphasized the long line, a concept that often dictates phrasing across the bar line to the next downbeat or further. When confronted by the short phrase or slurring patterns in these earlier works, 19th-century editors often adopted a practice whereby the patterns were simply changed by extending them to conform with long-line musical thinking. If questions were raised about taking this liberty, two arguments were usually put forward: the short phrase-slur marks were carryovers from a standard practice used in writing bowing for strings; and printing conventions and/or limitations of the period dictated ending phrases or slurring at the bar line.

In the mid-20th century scholars began to revisit this issue and to consider the possibility that perhaps these markings could not be dismissed quite so easily. Questions were raised that seemed to challenge traditional rationale. First, why would so many masters who were skilled keyboard players confuse keyboard techniques with string bowing to the extent of inserting bowing markings into their keyboard music, rather than markings that would assist the keyboard player? Second, how can one ascribe to period printing practice limitations that cursory observation proves did not exist? In other words, one can find many examples in early printed music where phrasing or slurring extends over the bar line, sometimes for several measures, sometimes stopping in the middle of measures. Finally, it should be noted that much slurring is not addressed by considerations of articulation vis–a–vis the bar line (for example, the frequently encountered two-note slurs in Beethoven).

Such speculation invites us to consider that perhaps much of the articulation was born of a touch sensitivity that came directly out of playing earlier keyboard instruments, such as the harpsichord and the fortepiano. In playing these instruments sustaining sound was not as important a consideration as it later became, since instruments of the time were limited in this regard. By the same token, refinement in executing individual note values and shorter phrase groups was more important as an expressive device. This focus led to a sensitivity of touch that allowed for the projection of various articulated groupings without destroying the longer musical thought, a sensitivity that was enhanced by the light action of the keyboards themselves. If today's keyboardists begin to look at the original phrase groups in this light, they will discover that it is quite possible to develop fingertip sensitivity to an extent that would permit honoring all of Beethoven's slurring with meticulous accuracy without impairing the longer musical thought.

---

[25] *Letters of Beethoven*, vol. III, pp. 1241–42.

Dynamics and Accents

Beethoven often repeats dynamic markings within the context of the same passage as a means of suggesting musical emphasis beyond the level of intensity directed by the dynamic itself. Since Beethoven was writing for the early piano, these duplicated dynamic markings do not serve the function of indicating which manual of a two-manual instrument each hand is to play upon. In recent editions that adapt such early keyboard music for the piano, many editors preserve only one of the duplicated dynamic indications.

To the contrary, Beethoven's repetition of dynamic marks seems to be a gesture meant to elicit a greater degree of emotional response on the part of the performer. As the player views and studies the music, the exhortation again and again to play *forte*, for example, is much the same as the emphatic gesture a conductor might use to incite ensemble musicians to more intense playing. Similarly, repeated reminders to play softly invites the performer to settle in to a mode of performance that effectively communicates the appropriate mood, be it one of tenderness, thoughtful contemplation, or prayerful meditation. Accordingly, Beethoven's dynamic repetitions are preserved by most editors, as they have been in this edition.

Beethoven uses a variety of markings to indicate accent: *sforzando*, *forte-piano* (or *fortissimo-piano*), *subito forte* (or *fortissimo*), *subito piano* (or *pianissimo*), wedges (vertical and horizontal), as well as the implied accent of *rinsforzando*, instituted by a re-enforced touch. In addition, certain ornaments invite accents, such as the initial note of a rapid mordent placed over the first note of a two-note slur (*Schneller*). Some form of such accent will be encountered by the performer in every movement of these sonatas, almost on every page. Thus, it becomes apparent that accents were of great importance to Beethoven, and meticulous realization of them is absolutely necessary for stylistic performance of this music.

Notwithstanding the importance of accents, there is much about their details of execution that remains elusive. Scholars have attempted without much success to discern a pattern of consistency in Beethoven's indications that would help determine how much accent is appropriate for a given symbol or in a given context. Although there has been a considerable amount of speculation and some attempts to codify Beethoven's symbols, no definitive guide has emerged and garnered widespread acceptance. Hence, exact interpretation and refinement of execution must be left to the performer. This responsibility, moreover, can be one of considerable complexity, for Beethoven uses accents in conjunction with metric accentuation, sometimes working with the strong beats of the meter, sometimes contrary to them (syncopation). In addition, the composer constantly employs elements of surprise in his music, suddenly accenting the unexpected or changing dynamic levels rapidly without warning. Studying these accents and arriving at a convincing execution of them are among the challenges that give Beethoven's music both its excitement and enduring vitality.

Ornamentation

Evidence exists that Beethoven was well acquainted with the 18th-century tradition of ornamentation that his generation inherited. Such a tradition is documented most clearly for keyboard players in the *Essay on the True Art of Playing Keyboard Instruments*[26] by Carl Philipp Emanuel Bach (1714–1788), a work published four times between the years 1753 and 1797. Czerny reported that he was asked to acquire this work when, at the age of 10, he began his lessons with Beethoven. By the same token, style in piano playing was undergoing profound change during Beethoven's lifetime and ornamentation was part of that process. By the middle of the 19th century, just a few decades after Beethoven's death, new ways of ornamentation were to be accepted as the norm by many musicians: trills beginning on the main note rather than the upper auxiliary; appoggiaturas and arpeggiation coming before the beat instead of on it; and ornamental flourishes of all kinds being written in ways that were increasingly exact and left less to the discretion of the performer.

Beethoven lived during the first echelon of this change. For example, in his friend Johann Nepomuk Hummel's *A Complete Theoretical and Practical Course of Instruction in the Art of Playing the Pianoforte...*, published in London and in Germany at about the time of Beethoven's death (1827), it is recommended that the trill start on the main note rather than the upper auxiliary.[27] To what extent Beethoven may have been influenced by Hummel's preference in this regard is unknown, as is whether or not Hummel was reflecting a practice that had become widespread by the time this method book was published. To these speculations must be added that Beethoven was, in fact, an innovator with regard to compositional techniques, forward looking and experimental. It stands to reason that, as a pianist, he would be as inventive and adventuresome in the performance of music, especially his own, and that he was probably not given much to letting tradition stand in the way of expression.

The journey of inquiry in this area is strewn with may attempts to find definitive answers to questions regarding the realization of ornaments. Among the many notable historic quests to solve the riddle of Beethoven ornamentation are those of Franz Kullak (1844–1913) in the book *Beethoven's Piano Playing, with an Essay on the Execution of the Trill*[28] (1881) and the Beethoven section of Edward Dannreuther's (1844–1905) two-volume work entitled *Musical Ornamentation*[29] (1893–95). Simultaneous with such research efforts was the building of a performance tradition in the hands of pianists who were

---

[26] Carl Philipp Emanuel Bach, *Essay on the True Art of Playing Keyboard Instruments*, trans. and ed. William J. Mitchell (New York: W. W. Norton, 1949).

[27] Johann Nepomuk Hummel, *Ausführlich theoretisch-practische Anweisung zum Piano-forte Spiel*, ca. 1822–25, second edition (Vienna: Tobias Haslinger, 1828), p. 394.

[28] Franz Kullak, *Beethoven's Piano Playing, with an Essay on the Execution of the Trill*, trans. Theodore Baker (New York: G. Schirmer, 1901).

[29] Edward Dannreuther, *Musical Ornamentation*. 2 volumes (London: Novello & Co., 1893–95).

great Beethoven specialists, such as Artur Schnabel (1882–1951). One can even point to a teacher-pupil lineage that moved from Beethoven to Czerny, from Czerny to Theodor Leschetizky (1830–1915), and from Leschetizky to a multitude 20th-century performers, including Schnabel. Much of the time the traditions built by famous performers favored 19th-century execution of ornaments notwithstanding the cautions tendered by researchers.

Such contradictory evidence should not be regarded as a license to avoid coming to grips with the problems. Some editors have realized ornamentation with strong allegiance to contemporary principles as set forth by C.P.E. Bach. These editors do not proceed very far, however, without encountering ornamentation for which exception to the contemporary practice seems to offer solutions that are more satisfying musically and/or more practical technically. Other editors adhere to some 19th-century performance traditions without apology. Still others offer suggestions for independent evaluation on the part of the performer. For example, William S. Newman in his excellent book *Performance Practices in Beethoven's Piano Sonatas*[30] (1971) suggests that the performer must decide how to execute each trill, taking into account harmony, melody, technical fluency, and rhythm. For this edition an attempt has been made to incorporate something of all of these approaches. Thus, a realization for an ornamentation problem is always offered, but this edition also often takes note of differing viewpoints, particularly in those cases where 18th-century performance practice and a later performing tradition diverge.

To summarize, the conclusion is inescapable that there are not always definitive answers to performance problems encountered in matters of articulation and ornamentation in the Beethoven sonatas. Each generation of performers, however, needs to address these issues anew, for continuing research engages us in an ongoing concentration on the details and values of the music. Such focus gives rise to personal conviction in playing the music, even in regard to the unfathomable, and creates a resurgence of vitality for present-day performance.

Tempo and Pulse in Beethoven's Music

Beethoven provided only general tempo directions in Italian or German at appropriate points in the score. In later works he refined these directions, in some instances by adding additional descriptive phrases. There is but a single exception to this practice, that being the metronome markings Beethoven left for the Op.106. This set of indications has been problematic, however, both for playing the Op. 106 itself and for providing a key with which to sense the composer's intentions regarding tempo in general, for the markings have been deemed by most musicians to be excessively fast. William S. Newman has even gone so far as to suggest that Beethoven's hearing loss had caused him to lose touch with the reality of physical execution as well as sound at that point in life.[31] Artur Schnabel's attempt to realize these metronome markings in a recording of the Op. 106 (ca. 1930) was well intentioned, to be sure, but the breathless, often scrambled impression the performance conveys has only served to support the contention that the indications are, indeed, much too fast for comfort and clarity.

Notwithstanding the limited directions from the composer himself, tempo and appropriate handling of pulse in performing Beethoven have been matters of both concern and debate from the earliest generation of scholars and performers to those of the present time. One of the most frequently cited sources on these subjects is Beethoven's early biographer Anton Schindler (1795–1864), who met the composer in 1814 and subsequently became his secretary and household assistant, intermittently until the composer's death in 1827. Schindler's biography of Beethoven underscores the composer's concern with tempo and describes Beethoven's performances of his own music in ways that suggest considerable latitude in both tempo and pulse regularity. For example, the 1840 edition of Schindler's biography of Beethoven contains a detailed account of the composer's performances of the two sonatas of Op. 14. The account focuses mostly on describing tempo changes and concludes that "*...in every moment Beethoven varied the tempo as the feelings changed.*"[32] Performers cannot,

---

[30] Newman, Op. cit., p. 52.

[31] Ibid., p. 52.

[32] Anton Felix Schindler, *Beethoven as I Knew Him*, vol. II, trans. Ignaz Moscheles (London: Henry Colburn, 1840), pp. 131–40. This account is also quoted by Harold Schonberg in *The Great Pianists* (New York: Simon & Schuster, 1963), pp. 79–84.

however, put too much credence in Schindler's descriptions, for he wrote them more than a decade after Beethoven's death. Moreover, Schindler's credibility and accuracy were seriously challenged even by his contemporaries, so much so that Schindler deleted most of the commentary on Beethoven's use of tempo and pulse from the final (third) edition of his Beethoven biography (1860).

Of the many 19th-century editions of the sonatas, the best-known ones that offer metronome markings are those of Czerny and Ignaz Moscheles (1794–1870). Czerny's markings appeared twice, first in an 1842 publication, then later in 1850, the later marks almost always faster, too fast in the opinions of many musicians. Later well-known editions that include metronome markings are those by Hans von Bülow (1830–1894), Artur Schnabel, and Alfredo Casella (1883–1947). Schnabel goes a step further by indicating changes in tempi within movements, reflecting his own interpretation and possibly Schindler's perception of Beethoven's performances. Schnabel's daring in this regard has, however, engendered considerable controversy among other pianists, many taking issue with not only the individual markings, but also the concept of suggesting fluctuations within movements. Many feel that, although it is possible that Schnabel's markings worked well for him, forging basic tempi and tempo fluctuations is a process that each individual must undertake during the process of performance preparation.

Moreover, recent thinking has become somewhat sophisticated regarding selecting tempi and suggests the tempo of a given performance may be influenced by a number of variables, including the sound of the performance instrument, the surrounding acoustics, and the sensibilities of the individual performer. Thus, it is not surprising that most recent editions eschew assigning metronome markings to the sonatas. Both setting basic tempi and effecting the subtle alterations of tempo in response to the flow of the music are dependent upon many elusive factors, not the least of which is the ability of the performer to project an individual point of view convincingly.

As a point of information, a sampling of metronome markings suggested by other editors has been provided in the following table. The editorial policy of this edition, however, will align itself the majority of recent critical editions by simply presenting Beethoven's tempo directions without elaboration, imprecise as those may be.

Part of a painting of Ludwig van Beethoven by W. J. Mähler, 1804
Archiv für Kunst und Geschichte, Berlin

Metronome Markings for Beethoven's Sonatas in This Volume

	Note Value	Casella	Czerny 1842	Czerny 1850	Moscheles	Bülow	Schnabel	Taylor
Op. 31, No. 1								
Allegro vivace	♩ =	168	144	152	160	138	160	144–152
Adagio grazioso	♪ =	138	116	126	132	112	112	112
Allegretto	𝅗𝅥 =	108	96	100	84	80	100	96
Op. 31, No. 2								
Largo	♩ =	48	-	50	50	44	60	52
Allegro	𝅗𝅥 =	116	104	108	126	108	120	108
Adagio	♩ =	60	42	46	46	50	44	46–48
Allegretto	♩. =	84	76	88	88	80	69	69
Op. 31, No. 3								
Allegro	♩ =	120–126	144	152	160	116	116	120
Allegretto vivace	♩ =	92–96	80	88	92	100	100	92
Moderato e grazioso	♩ =	104–108	88	96	112	88	96	96
Presto con fuoco	𝅗𝅥. =	108	100	96	96	84	100	96
Op. 49, No. 1								
Andante	♩ =	80–84	-	60	-	60	66	69
Allegro	♩. =	112	-	60	-	92	112–120	108
Op. 49, No. 2								
Allegro, ma non troppo	𝅗𝅥 =	84–88	-	104	-	66	88	80–84
Tempo di Menuetto	♩ =	112–116	-	112	-	112	120	120
Op. 53								
Allegro con brio	♩ =	168–176	176	176	176	168	176	152
Adagio molto	♪ =	60	56	60	60	60	44	46
Allegretto moderato	♩ =	108–112	88	100	112	108	112	104
Prestissimo	𝅝 =	76–80	88	84	80	76	88	76
Op. 54								
In Tempo d'un Menuetto	♩ =	104–108	108	108	120	104	104	104
Allegretto	♩ =	138	144	120	108	138–144	126	126
Op. 57								
Allegro assai	♩. =	126	108	120	126	126	120	-
Andante con moto	♪ =	100	108	112	92	100–108	96	-
Allegro, ma non troppo	♩ =	138–144	132	144	152	132–138	152	-
Presto	𝅗𝅥 =	92–96	-	96	100	92–96	104	-
Op. 78								
Adagio cantabile	♪ =	80	72	76	76	72	63	63
Allegro, ma non troppo	♩ =	138	116	138	138	126	126	120–126
Allegro vivace	♩ =	144	132	132	132	138	152	138

About the Op. 31 Set

Op. 31 title page from the N. Simrock first edition, reproduced by kind permission from the copy in the Austrian National Library, Hoboken Collection, S. H. Beethoven 171

From April to October 1802, Beethoven lived in the small town of Heiligenstadt, just north of Vienna. During his stay, he received a request from the Zurich publisher Hans Georg Nägeli (1773–1836) for three sonatas, to be included in a series entitled *Répertoire des Clavicinistes*. Beethoven negotiated a fee of one hundred ducats for the set and immediately began to write the works. As they neared completion, Beethoven's brother Carl (1774–1815), then acting as a secretary for the composer, tried to get Ludwig to send the sonatas to a publisher in Leipzig, presumably for more money, but the composer honored his agreement with Nägeli and asked his lifelong Ferdinand Ries (1784–1838) to send the works to the Swiss publisher.

In the late spring of 1803, the first two sonatas of the set were returned to Beethoven in their published form, the composer never having seen proofs. As he went over the works, the composer counted nearly 80 errors. Beethoven instructed his brother to issue a statement to a professional journal, *Allegemeine musikalische*, announcing that the new sonatas contained many errors. Moreover, he asked Ries to prepare a list of errors, sending both the list and the new works to the Bonn publisher Nikolaus Simrock (1751–1832) for re-publication. In the fall of 1803, Simrock's publication appeared with the addendum: *Editiou* (sic) *tres correcte*. Simrock published the two sonatas of the set in 1803, the third in 1804, and finally all three together in 1805. The Viennese engraver Giovanni Cappi (1765–1815) also published the three sonatas together in 1805, erroneously as Op. 29.

Autographs of the three sonatas are not extant. One might assume that in dealing with the two "first" editions, one would be safe in discounting the Nägeli and relying on the Simrock edition. Recent research, however, has suggested that such an assumption is simplistic, for the Simrock also shows inconsistencies and possible errors.

Up to this point, there had been no dedication in connection with these works. According to the French musicologist Jacques Gabriel Prod'homme (1871–1956), the Cappi publica

tion was dedicated to Countess Anna Margarete von Browne, wife of Count Johann Georg von Browne (1767–1827). The couple had been patrons of Beethoven during the 1790s, reportedly having presented the composer with a horse at one point. The Countess was believed to have been an excellent pianist. Beethoven also dedicated the Op. 10 piano sonatas to her. The dedication of the Op. 31 set to the Countess has not been verified, however, and thus does not appear in most editions of the works.

Beethoven's sketchbooks suggest that the Op. 31, No. 2 was conceived earlier than No. 1. Moreover, No. 1 was originally sketched for string quartet, although the composer abandoned that version early on.

The attachment of the nickname "Tempest" to the Op. 31, No. 2 sonata comes from Beethoven's student and assistant Anton Felix Schindler (1795–1864). Schindler comments on Czerny's performances of the Op. 31, No. 2, and the Op. 57 sonatas, and pressed the composer to *"give me the key to these sonatas."* According to Schindler, Beethoven replied, *"Just read Shakespeare's Tempest."*[33] Recent research has tended to discredit the accuracy of Schindler's accounts and, as noted above, he asked about two sonatas, not just the Op. 31, No. 2. Still, the designation "Tempest" has become firmly rooted in the professional culture as the nickname for Op. 31, No. 2.

---

[33] Anton Felix Schindler, *Beethoven as I Knew Him*, ed. Donald W. McArdle, trans. Constance S. Jolly (Chapel Hill: University of North Carolina Press, 1966), p. 406. This book is based on Schindler's 1860 revision of his own earlier 1840 version and is available in reprint from Dover Publications, Mineola, NY.

Sonata No. 16 in G Major, Op. 31, No. 1

Autograph/facsimile:	lost
Sketches/loose pages:	yes
First editions:	Nägeli: Zurich, late spring 1803
	N. Simrock: Bonn, fall 1803

The first sonata of the Op. 31 set is one of Beethoven's most jovial, filled with both original and humorous touches.

Its first movement, marked *Allegro vivace*, is cast in a traditional sonata-allegro form, the exposition marked to be repeated. The first theme area (measures 1–65) opens with material that combines a descending run with syncopated chords, the right hand preceding the left by only a sixteenth note. Could the composer be making fun of performers with an inability to play hands together? This opening idea is then repeated a whole step lower, foreshadowing the more famous use of this device in the opening of the Op. 53. The second theme area (measures 66–113) opens with a syncopated theme in the key of B major, the submediant of the home key, once again foreshadowing the Op. 53 with its use of the mediant as a key for the second theme area. The composer seems to vacillate, however, between the major mode and its parallel minor, the exposition coming to rest in B minor. The development section (measures 114–192) utilizes both the syncopated chords and passagework from the first theme area of the exposition. The recapitulation (upbeat to measure 194–278) presents all the material heard in the exposition. The first theme area is shortened (upbeat to measure 194–217). Although the second theme area (measures 218–278) opens in the mediant key of E major, it moves to the home key of G major (measure 234), from that point on using it as a base from which to mount short excursions into other keys. The coda (measures 279–325) is very funny, opening with a restatement of the first theme, but settling into dominant gestures (at the upbeat to measure 296), made tentative and unable to come to rest on the tonic by the use of rests and soft dynamic levels. A surprise *ff* (upbeat to measure 320–322) followed by a final timid tonic marked *p* (measure 324) is almost sure to evoke a chuckle from an audience.

The second movement is one of only three in the sonatas that makes use of a $\frac{9}{8}$ time signature. Marked *Adagio grazioso*, its barcarolle-like flow is both elegant and breathtaking, filled with elaborate ornamental gestures, a parade of trills, grace notes, passage work, double notes, and cadenzas. Its essential structure is **A B A** with a coda.

The opening **A** section (measure 1 through the downbeat of 35) presents its own short departure (upbeat to measure 17–26) with a cadenza leading back to a restatement of the opening idea (measure 27 through the downbeat of 35). The **B** section (measures 35–64) seemingly opens in the key of C minor, but moves almost immediately to A-flat major, and features a long sustained line over a sixteenth-note accompaniment. This supporting figuration is carried over as an accompaniment for the return of **A** (at measure 65). The coda (measures 99–119) continues to employ elaborate ornamentation right up to the quiet conclusion of the movement.

The final movement presents a typical Rondo pattern: **A B A C A B** with the final return of return of **A** being fragmented and leading to a humorous coda, marked *Presto*.

The opening **A** section (through the downbeat of 42) presents a lyrical theme, first in the right hand and then in the left hand. A transitional section (upbeat to measure 25 through the downbeat of 42) uses fragments of the opening theme in a development-like fashion. The first **B** section (measures 42–66) is in the dominant key (D major) and features triplets used both thematically and as a tremolo accompaniment to staccato chords (starting at measure 54). At the return of **A** (upbeat to measure 67), the main theme begins to be altered (upbeat to measure 75) so that the parallel minor (G minor) begins to play a prominent role. Such alterations lead seamlessly to the **C** section, which is, in fact, a development section that makes use of both first and second theme material (upbeat to measure 87 through the upbeat to 133). Thus the movement acts very much like a sonata-allegro structure, although the composers himself dubs it a Rondo. The return of **A** (upbeat to measure 133 through the downbeat of 178) leads to a restatement of **B**, now in the tonic (at measure 178). The final return of **A** is delayed by another development-like extension (upbeat to measure 207 through the upbeat to 225). When it does return, it is fragmented by rests and tempo changes (upbeat to measure 225–242). A bass trill at measure 241 ushers in the final *Presto*, a section based on the upbeat figure of the main theme. As in the first movement of this work, the composer uses rests and surprise dynamic changes to generate humor as the work closes (measures 262–275).

Sonata No. 17 in D Minor, Op. 31, No. 2

Autograph/facsimile:	lost
Sketches/loose pages:	yes
First edition:	Nägeli: Zurich, late spring 1803
	N. Simrock: Bonn, fall 1803

The second sonata of the Op. 31 is one of the composer's best known, justly deserving its popularity by containing a dramatic opening movement, a profound slow movement, and a perpetual-motion type final movement. The first and final movements are in a traditional sonata-allegro form, and the slow movement is a sonata-allegro without a development (sometimes referred to as "truncated").

A *Largo* opens the first movement (measures 1–2) and serves as both an introduction and a solemn statement of the motive that reappears throughout the movement. A second idea (upbeat to measure 3–6) presents rapid, descending couplets. The introductory motive, now *Allegro*, returns as part of the first theme area (measures 21–22; 25–26; 29–30, etc.). The second theme area (measures 41–96) is in the dominant minor and initially sets forth material derived from the previously mentioned couplets (measures 41–54). The exposition (marked to be repeated) moves into the development (measures 97–147) with a reiteration of the opening motive, once again *Largo*, then *Allegro*. The recapitulation (measures 147–232) also makes uses of *Largo*, now expanded to two passages that extend the opening motive into short recitatives. A short extension of the final tonic brings the movement to a quiet conclusion.

The exposition of the second movement (measures 1–42) opens with a meditative theme that contrasts chorale-like chords with a short dotted-rhythm motive presented in high registers (measures 1 through the downbeat of 17). An important transitional theme (measures 17 through the downbeat of 30) features a choral melody over a drum-like tremolo bass figure. A lyrical second theme (measure 30 through the downbeat of 38) in the dominant (F major) leads to a closing section (measures 38–42) derived from the transitional theme. In measure 42, the exposition ends and modulates back to the key of B-flat, ushering in the recapitulation (measure 43 through the downbeat of 89). The recapitulation reiterates all events of the exposition with some elaboration, notably the left-hand arpeggios that accompany the opening theme (measure 51 through the downbeat of 59). A coda (measures 89–103) is based primarily on the opening theme and effectively employs contrasting registers of the keyboard.

The final movement draws its energy from the fact that sixteenth notes permeate virtually every measure. Its exposition (upbeat to measure 1–94), is marked to be repeated and, like the first movement, presents second theme material in the dominant minor (A minor) (measures 43–94). A lengthy development (upbeat to measure 95 to the upbeat to 215) is based entirely on first theme material, except for a possible short reference to the second theme motive (measures 169–173) in the upper voice of the right hand. The recapitulation (upbeat to measure 215 through the first half of 322) is regular, remaining in the home key, and leads to an extended coda, still based on the main theme (upbeat to measure 323–399), but one that opens much the same way as the development section had opened. A final descending arpeggio brings this driving movement to its conclusion.

Sonata No. 18 in E-flat Major, Op. 31, No. 3

Autograph/facsimile:	lost
Sketches/loose pages:	yes
First edition:	Nägeli: Zurich, late spring 1803
	N. Simrock: Bonn, fall 1803

Although this sonata is cast in four movements, it does not follow the more traditional four-movement arrangement of many of the earlier sonatas, for it has no slow movement, substituting instead a lively scherzo as the second movement and a minuet and trio as the third. Moreover, three of the four movements are cast in sonata-allegro form, an atypical concentration of a single structure within the framework of a sonata.

The opening sonority of the first movement, marked *Allegro*, has become well known, for it is seemingly ambiguous in its harmonic function. It is soon revealed as a first inversion of the supertonic in E-flat major (measures 1–8). The progression leading to its resolution becomes a hallmark of the movement, seemingly having delighted the composer, for he uses it as a first theme, and it continues to be prominent in the development, recapitulation, and coda. The second theme area, including the closing theme (upbeat to measure 46–88) is presented traditionally in the dominant (B-flat). The exposition is marked to be repeated. The development section (measures 89–136) states and expands on the opening idea of the movement, and the recapitulation (measures 137–219) is regular, leading directly to a coda (measures 220–253), which expands and restates the opening idea once again.

The composer calls the second movement *Scherzo*, marked *Allegretto vivace*, notwithstanding the fact that it is in duple meter and in sonata allegro form. Clearly, he uses the term to indicate the spirit of the movement rather than one linked to an enlivened minuet and trio, as in previous sonatas. The movement is compact and jovial. It opens with material that contrasts a cheerful theme accompanied by staccato sixteenth notes with suspenseful monophonic recitative-like interruptions (measures 1–34). Non-stop sixteenth notes characterize the second theme in the dominant key (upbeat to measure 35 through the downbeat of 50) and again serve as an accompaniment for the closing theme (measures 50–61). The exposition is marked to be repeated. The development section makes use of both the first and second themes (measures 64–107), and the recapitulation is regular with a short extension of the closing theme acting as a coda (measures 108–173).

The menuetto and trio, marked *Moderato e grazioso*, is completely regular in its structure other than the fact that the *da capo* is written out, presumably to ensure that both sections are repeated in the return, as marked, rather than playing them without repeats as would be customary. A short coda closes the movement (measures 60–68).

The final *Presto con fuoco* movement features non-stop triplet rhythm, presenting either eighth note triplets, or broken triplets (with a rest on the second of the three). This driving energy has resulted in many musicians referring to the movement as a "tarantella." Its sonata-allegro structure is very compact, the opening section of the exposition presenting an opening theme with a triplet accompaniment (measures 1–12) and a transitional theme based on broken triplets (upbeat to measure 13–33). The second theme is in the dominant key (F), and opens with the triplets once again acting as an accompaniment to a repeated note motive in the RH (measures 34–63). The short closing theme (measures 64–79) is related to the transitional theme through its use of broken triplets. The exposition is marked to be repeated. The development section (measures 82–166) makes use of ideas related to both types of triplet figurations. The recapitulation (beginning at the upbeat to measure 174) is regular up until its second theme (beginning at measure 211) which is unexpectedly presented in the key of G-flat major. This continues into the closing theme (beginning at measure 241), which is extended, but ends up suddenly on the dominant of the home key (measure 265). A coda follows, featuring the opening theme restated and expanded (measures 282–335), and providing a lively, brilliant ending for the sonata.

Sonata No. 16 in G Major

Ludwig van Beethoven (1770–1827)
Op. 31, No. 1

ⓐ Note that if the performer takes the repeat at the end of measure 113, the G in measure 3 should be played *f*.

ⓑ The RH stretches in measures 93–95 and 261–263 are difficult at best and impossible for small hands. Martienssen, Tovey, Schnabel, and Taylor suggest facilitation through these passages as exemplified by measure 93:

Casella and Schnabel also suggest the following alternative:

ⓒ In Nägeli, the marking for the RH entrance in measure 140 is ***f***, but the entrance in 148 is ***sf***. In Simrock, both entrances are marked ***f***. Nine of the referenced editors change the marking in measure 140 to ***sf***. The remaining four (and this editor) prefer to follow Simrock.

ⓓ Eight of the referenced editors offer comment on the trills in measures 141 and 149, all in agreement with starting on the main note. There is, however, disagreement as to whether to add after-notes (*nachschlag*). D'Albert, Arrau, Schenker, and Schnabel recommend their use, and Bülow, Casella, and Taylor eschew them. Tovey suggests not using them in his notes, then adds them in parentheses in the score (perhaps Craxton made the addition). Executing seven notes (including after-notes) is difficult at tempo. Schenker suggests a five-note figure (with the after-notes), which seems sufficient. Schnabel provides the following facilitation:

measure 141:

(e) The Nägeli first edition shows four added measures after measure 298:

According to Ferdinand Ries, this addition especially infuriated the composer.

(a) Of the nine referenced editors whose fingering indicates where to begin the trills that open and appear throughout this movement (measures 1, 3, 9, 11, 27, 29, 65, 67, 73, 75, 91, and 93), eight start on the main note each time, a realization with which this editor agrees. Only Arrau indicates starting on the upper note, and then only when the theme is in the RH. When the LH plays the theme, the trill is always preceded by one or more grace notes; in these cases, Arrau begins the trill on the main note (measures 9, 11, 73, and 75). Only Bülow attempts to write out the trill, using sextuplet thirty-second notes for each triplet eighth in the LH, ending with a five-note figure that incorporates Beethoven's written-out after-notes (*nachschlag*). Bülow allows the sextuplets to be subdivided into thirty-second-note triplets when the LH has sixteenth notes at the return of the theme in measure 65, but only as long as it takes to gain coordination of the hands, advising the player to return to thirty-second sextuplets as soon as possible.

(b) Casella, Taylor, and Tovey express concern that the staccato notes resemble string pizzicato, thus not being too short or dry. Casella pedals the entire first beat of each measure. Tovey suggests "limited" pedal. Taylor refers only to sensitivity of touch.

(c) The Nägeli first edition renders measure 5 as follows:

All of the referenced editors have assumed this to be an example of the many errors Beethoven complained about in the Nägeli edition and have followed the presentation that appeared in the Simrock edition, one that the composer presumably endorsed. The Simrock version brings measure 5 into conformity with measure 69. It can be noted, however, that Beethoven varies the idea in both measures 31 and 95, thus opening up the question as to whether or not the Nägeli rendition might possibly be valid.

A second issue is the notation of grace notes such as those in measure 5. Both Nägeli and Simrock use sixteenth and thirty-second notes for the most part throughout the movement. Arrau, Hauschild, Krebs, Schenker, Taylor, and Wallner have preserved this notation. The other referenced editors render all grace notes as eighth notes with a slash across the stem. Only two of the referenced editors offer advice with regard to their execution. In measure 5, Schnabel indicates playing the grace notes before the beat. Taylor suggests playing grace notes on the beat. This editor agrees with Taylor.

The fingering indications 1 3 1 3 1 3 here and in measure 74 appear only in Simrock, but are presumed to be by the composer.

(e) Only four of the referenced editors provide fingering for this trill. They all start on the main note and add after-notes (*nachschlag*). Arrau and Taylor use six notes:

(f) Trill fingering from seven editors suggest starting on the main note. Arrau and Wallner (1980 only) show fingering that starts on the upper note. Several editors comment that the trill should flow into the cadenza. Several editors also suggest dividing the cadenza. Bülow indicates light accents on notes that outline the dominant seventh harmony (9, 15, 22, 30, 38), then on notes 42 and 49. Groupings starting on notes 38, 42, and 49 are also shown by Taylor. Tovey suggests groups of eight notes, slowing down for the last group of six thirty-second notes and flowing into the following eighth notes. Casella writes out an individual grouping that can be shown only by reproducing it:

(g) The E in the LH is missing in both Nägeli and Simrock, but all of the referenced editors except Hauschild add it so that this measure conforms to measure 5.

ⓗ Schnabel and Taylor recommend playing double grace notes rapidly on the beat, as well as those in the following section (measures 42, 44, 46, and 48). The accent, however, should remain on the main note in each case. This editor prefers the grace notes before the beat.

(i) Slurring across the bar line between measures 87 and 88, as well as 88 and 89, occurs in both Nägeli and Simrock, making the articulation different from that in measures 23–24 and 24–25. Bülow, Casella, Kohler, Schnabel, and Tovey present both places with across-the-bar phrasing. Schenker renders both with phrases ending at bar lines. D'Albert, Arrau, Hauschild, Krebs, Martienssen, Taylor, and Wallner preserve the differentiated slurring.

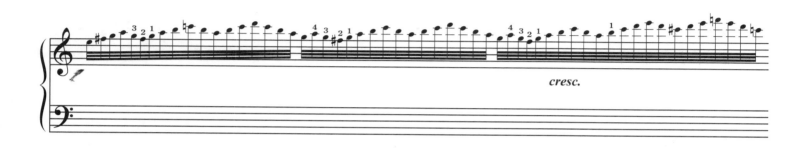

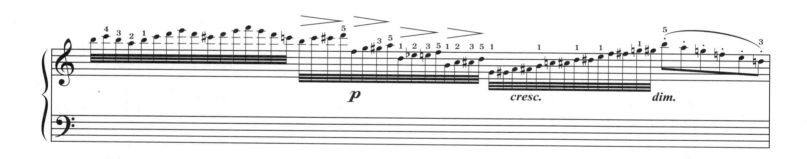

ⓙ The beams for this cadenza are the same in both Nägeli and Simrock. Although the groups contain irregular numbers of thirty-second notes (23, 18, 16, 22, 16, 16, 14), they nevertheless outline shapes that convey the musical idea behind the cadenza, surging upward twice to the high F, probably the highest note on Beethoven's keyboard. Bülow suggests accenting the notes that outline the dominant seventh chord (3, 7, 13, 19, 26, 32, 38, etc.). Casella, as in the first cadenza, creates a similar effect by writing out his own groupings:

(k) Bülow's suggestion of breaking this figure into ♪♪♪♪ + ♪♪♪♪ + ♪♪♪ is not appropriate in the opinion of this editor. Taylor suggests "scanning" the figure as 4+4+3, but playing the groups "as evenly as possible."

(l) Almost all of the referenced editors agree that the trills in measures 99 and 100, as well as those in measures 104 and 105, should start on main notes. Only Tovey calls for the upper note on the downbeats of measures 99 and 104 (presumably because of the final sixteenth note of the preceding measure in each case). Bülow writes out the trills as sextuplet sixteenth notes. Both Nägeli and Simrock show after-notes (*nachschlag*) for all of the trills in measures 104 and 105, but none in measures 99 and 100. D'Albert, Arrau, Casella, Schenker, Schnabel, and Tovey recommend adding them.

(m) Twelve of the referenced editors indicate using B-flat as the upper note of the first trill. Casella argues for the B-natural, not only because no indication of B-flat is in either Nägeli or Simrock, but also because he deems the harmony to be functioning in the key of C major, pointing to the other B-naturals in the same measure. The referenced editors all agree that these trills begin on the main note. Bülow suggests a seven-note figure, a workable solution:

(n) An erroneous tradition exists of placing a *p* in measure 108, sometimes preceded by a diminuendo indication in measure 107. These indications do not appear in either Nägeli or Simrock. D'Albert, Bülow, Kohler, Martienssen, and Schenker make this error, while Arrau, Casella, Schnabel, Taylor, and Tovey point to the error and advise continuing with the *f* of measure 106. Wallner puts it in parenthesis in her 1953 edition, but deletes in the 1980 printing.

The LH trills in measures 108 and 110 should begin on the main note according to the fingering of all of the referenced editors except Arrau, who reverts to his preference for beginning trills on the upper note on the downbeats of both measures. As before, Bülow suggests sextuplet thirty-second notes, incorporating the after-notes (*nachschlag*) in the last set.

Nägeli and Simrock present different patterns of sforzandi in measures 111, 112, and 113. Both place the *sf* on the LH G in measure 111. Nägeli shows two *sf* marks in measure 112, one on the LH A-flat on beat 4, and one on the RH F on beat 5, repeating only the RH mark in measure 113. In both measures 112 and 113, Simrock shows one *sf* midway between the staves on beat 5. This array of inconsistencies has been resolved in most of the referenced editions by placing *sf* signs on the LH A-flats in all three measures, and on the RH F's on beat 5 in measures 112 and 113. Only Taylor and Wallner footnote the problem. The text of this edition has combined the marks in Nägeli and Simrock, adding nothing else.

RONDO

Allegretto

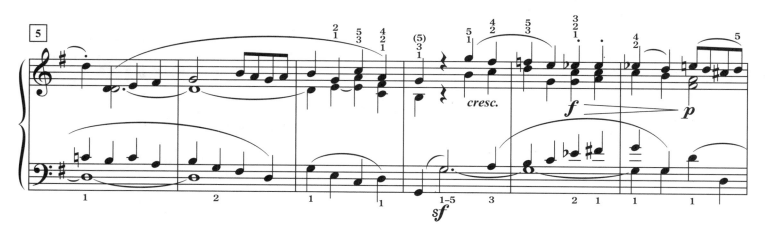

(a) The grace note in this thematic figure is written throughout the movement as a small eighth note with a slash across its stem in Nägeli, and as a small sixteenth note (without a slash) in Simrock. Editors are divided almost equally as to which notation to follow, and none addresses execution. This editor recommends playing these grace notes very rapidly before the beat.

(b) The phrasing of the opening theme is erratic in both Nägeli and Simrock, the theme being presented with a variety of slurring patterns on reappearances throughout the movement. The most noticeable issue is whether or not the slur crosses the bar line at measures 4 and 7, thus making the downbeats of measures 5 and 8 the end of the phrase or to play it as a rhythmic beginning against which the *sf*s are to be played. Similar spots are at measures 19–20, 23–24, 69–70, 73–74, 85–86, 135–136, 139–140, 151–152, and 155–156. Nägeli shows slurs crossing bar lines only at measures 151–152 and 155–156. Simrock presents no discernable pattern, showing crossing at measures 3–4, 19–20, 73–74, 139–140, 151–152, and 155–156, six times in all, but not crossing at measures 7–8, 23–24, 69–70, 85–86, and 135–136, five times. Editors have presented a variety of patterns. Older editions show allegiance to the nineteenth-century preference for longer lines, and these editions cross the bar lines in all instances: Bülow, Casella, Kohler, Tovey, and Schnabel. Krebs reproduces the Nägeli slurring; d'Albert, Martienssen, and Schenker each present different individual realizations, none with apparent logic. Four more recent editors—Arrau, Hauschild, Taylor, and Wallner—appear to reproduce the patterns presented in Simrock, correcting two mistakes in the process, but offering no comment on the inconsistencies. This editor joins the latter group, pointing to the problem but preferring to let the interpreter choose how to realize the score.

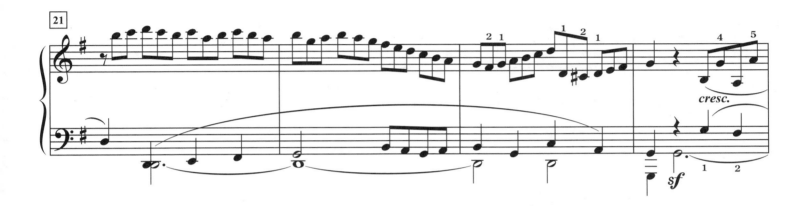

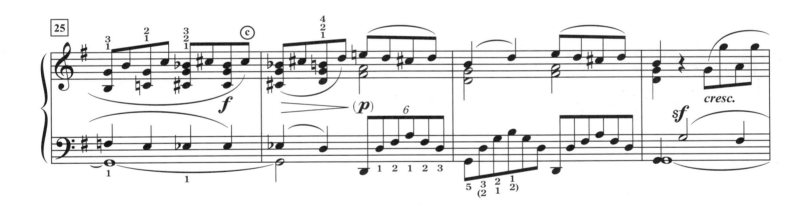

ⓒ The RH articulation in measures 25 and 26 is represented as it appears in both Nägeli and Simrock. Only d'Albert, Bülow, Krebs, and Martienssen follow these sources. The remaining referenced editors extend the slur that begins on the second half of measure 24 through to the second half of measure 26.

ⓓ Small hands may have to arpeggiate the intervals of the ninth that appear in the LH in measures 30, 31, 162, and 163, as well as the one in the RH in measure 94. If so, play the lower note rapidly before the beat.

48

50

ⓔ The editorial articulation in measures 208, 210, and 211 appear in neither Nägeli or Simrock, but ten of the referenced editors (and this editor) suggest all or part of it.

(f) Fingering from all of the referenced editors who deal with this trill indicates starting it on the main note. This editor agrees.
The speed of the trill can be that of the eighth note in the *Presto*.

Sonata No. 17 in D Minor

Ludwig van Beethoven (1770–1827)
Op. 31, No. 2

(a) Both Nägeli and Simrock show ¢. Bülow and Köhler erroneously show C. Pedal indications throughout the movement are in both first editions.

(b) Bülow, Casella, and Schnabel offer realizations for this turn:

Bülow and Casella:

Schnabel:

(c) Bülow shows a disposition between the hands that is frequently recommended, that of continuing to play the triplet eighth notes with the RH and crossing over with the LH to play the melody in the treble clef in measures 22–24 and 26–28, using the damper pedal to sustain whole notes in the bass. This results in some degree of blurring in measures 23 and 27. Tovey and Casella permit crossing in measures 30, 32, 34, 36, and 38–40, where use of the damper pedal does not blur the line, but compromises the staccato marked on the *sf* quarter notes in measures 30, 32, 34, and 36. D'Albert, Schenker, and Schnabel recommend crossing only in measures 38–40, where the *sf* quarter notes no longer carry a staccato mark (both in Nägeli and Simrock). This editor agrees with crossing in measures 38–40, where the eighth-note triplet figure is high enough to make playing it with the LH awkward.

56

(d) The pedal markings in measures 147–152 and 157 through the downbeat of 163 are shown in both Nägeli and Simrock. Only d'Albert, Bülow, and Köhler change these markings. The remaining referenced editors follow the first editions, Casella and Schnabel pointing to the special pedal effect in footnotes. For those who find using full pedal objectionable, Taylor and Tovey suggest in their editions to hold the LH chord down and use discreet half-damping in the recitatives as a possibility. Charles Rosen also suggests this in his book on the sonatas. (*Beethoven's Piano Sonatas: A Short Companion*; Yale University Press; New Haven, 2002, footnote on page 170.) William S. Newman argues that the taste for color blurring was evidenced not only by Beethoven, but also by several composers of the period. (Newman: *Beethoven on Beethoven: Playing His Piano Music His Way*; W. W. Norton; New York; 1988; pp. 245–46.) Moreover, Newman traces anecdotal documentation through five parties that the composer stated he wanted the passage to sound like a voice in a vault.

(e) Both Nägeli and Simrock print the note D-flat as the final sixteenth note in measure 159. However, the note is changed to C in a copy from the collection of the *Gesellschaft der Musikfreunde* (Society of Friends of Music). This society was founded in Vienna in 1812 and holds one of the most important historic music collections in the world. An early acquisition came from the estate of Beethoven's lifelong friend the Archduke Rudolf (1788–1831). Thus, the change in measure 159 is reputed to have been made by Beethoven himself. Of the referenced editors, nine print the D-flat without comment and five print C or offer it as an alternative, Hauschild, Taylor, and Wallner providing notes.

ⓕ Both Nägeli and Simrock divide the arpeggios in measures 165–166 and 169–170 between two staves, almost identically. The referenced editors are almost equally divided in the disposition of these arpeggios, six opting for execution of both by the RH only, five suggesting a variety of ways to divide the arpeggios between the hands. In this editor's opinion, the arpeggio in measures 165–166 can be executed comfortably with the RH. The one in measures 169–170 is more awkward, so the player might want to consider the following division:

measures 169–170:

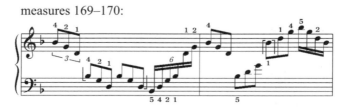

(g) The range limitation of Beethoven's keyboard forced him to write the RH of measures 193–196 differently from that of measures 59–62. Ten of the referenced editors present Beethoven's version without comment. Köhler offers an alternative version that is a transposition of measures 59–62. Casella refers to the possibility of such transposition in a footnote, but advises against it. This editor prefers to use the composer's version.

64

(a) Only Bülow offers advice with regard to this arpeggiation, suggesting it be slow with the uppermost note occurring on the downbeat.

(b) Schnabel and d'Albert recommend the following:

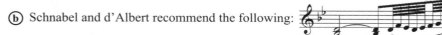

Bülow starts the run earlier; his notation suggests incorporating some degree of freedom:

Both Taylor and Tovey in written commentary suggest starting the run somewhere after the last quarter beat, but before the last eighth beat of the measure.

(c) Of the referenced editors, ten indicate by fingering that the trill begins on the main note. Arrau's fingering suggests starting on the upper auxiliary. Bülow provides a practical realization:

 Apply also to measure 50.

(d) Disagreement is evidenced among the referenced editors as to how to execute the turn figure that appears in measures 10, 12, 14, 44, 46, 48, 52, 54, 56, 93, and 95. Arrau, Casella, Martienssen, Schenker, Schnabel, and Tovey recommend either of the following:

measure 10:

d'Albert, Bülow, Köhler, and Taylor realize the figure as follows:

measure 10:

Schnabel states that he does not like the first realization preferred by the second group as it "falsifies the rhythmic form." Taylor, on the other hand, argues that the realizations preferred by the first group "ignore Beethoven's important tie." Although seemingly a close call, this editor sides with the second group.

Interestingly, the two first editions show different placements of the turn sign, Nägeli placing it over the dotted sixteenth note in each case, and Simrock between the dotted sixteenth and the ensuing thirty-second note. (Nägeli's engraver slips once in measure 10, but otherwise the sign is represented as stated.)

ⓔ The turn symbol appears over the tied C on beat 2 in both Nägeli and Simrock. D'Albert, Arrau, Schnabel, and Taylor show realizations that begin after beat 2:

Schnabel and Taylor: d'Albert: Arrau:

Bülow, Casella, Köhler, Martienssen, Schenker, and Tovey opt for a version of the turn beginning before beat 2:

either: or:

Bülow acknowledges the first edition notation in a footnote, but deems its literal realization "doubtless not intended."
This editor joins the first group and prefers literal reading of the first edition.

ⓕ In both Nägeli and Simrock, measure 27 shows a slur in the RH between the first two chords. There is no slur in any of the subsequent figures in measures 28 and 29, nor in the repeat of the passage at measures 69, 70, and 71. Editors have addressed this inconsistency differently. Eight of the referenced editors simply apply the slur shown in measure 27 to all subsequent measures. Arrau, Krebs, Taylor, and Wallner apply the slur in measure 27 to measure 69, but leave the other measures (28, 29, 70, and 71) without slurs. Schenker places slurs in measures 27, 28, 69, and 70, but leaves the slurs off in measures 29 and 71. This editor has followed the pattern of the second group.

(g) Some performers may find interest in a tradition of rearranging the hands in measures 51, 53, and 55 so that they are not required to cross. Attributed to Adlof Henselt (1814–1889), this version was reproduced by Karl Klindworth (1830–1916) in his edition of the sonatas, and can be seen as an alternative in Casella's edition.

(h) Bülow suggests starting this run on beat 3 of the measure. D'Albert and Schnabel prefer to wait until immediately after the second half of beat 3.

(i) Of the editors whose indications are clear, nine start the trills in measures 100 and 101 on the main note. Arrau recommends the upper note, and Bülow uses the upper note in measure 100 (undoubtedly because of the immediately preceding D) and the main note in measure 101. Six indicate using after-notes (*nachschlag*) for each, and Schnabel prefers not using after-notes. This editor recommends the following:

(a) The low E that would allow the F in measure 42 to resolve downward was undoubtedly not available on Beethoven's piano. Bülow, Casella, Köhler, and Tovey indicate using it on today's piano. The other nine referenced editors and this one prefer following the first edition.

(b) In a historical context, this ornament when used by Beethoven is referred to as a *Pralltriller*. The composer typically applies it to the first note of a descending stepwise figure, notating it as a short mordent without a slash. Realizations of the figure should begin on the main note, on the beat, and its execution should be with a rhythmic cohesion that renders the figure more incisive than a melodic triplet does. This effect can be achieved by applying a strong accent to the first note:

measure 43:

At tempo, a rapid triplet with an accented downbeat will probably be the only execution possible. However, editors have warned against the figure sounding like a melodic triplet rather than a snappy ornament. Schnabel uses the above notation. Bülow and Taylor try to capture its effect with the following:

or:

This editor recommends the realization just described.

In this specific spot, however, Czerny writes out a realization that departs from the norm:

He gives his reason for such a departure as, "the bass note must come out smartly after the two small notes." (*Carl Czerny: On the Proper Performance of Beethoven's Works for the Piano*; edited with commentary by Paul Badura-Skoda; Universal Editions; Vienna, 1970, p. 44.) Incidentally, Czerny's realization is also easier to coordinate for many performers. Casella adopts Czerny's version. Tovey recommends the awkward combination of starting the ornament on the beat but accenting the third note of each figure. (See also Vol. I of this edition, p. 222, footnote (f).)

72

ⓒ Both Nägeli and Simrock show the *p* mark on the downbeat of measure 73. However, measure 301, the analogous measure in the recapitulation, shows the *p* on beat 2 of the measure. This difference has led eleven of the referenced editors to deem measure 73 in error and change it to match measure 301. Only Wallner takes note of the change. Schenker and Taylor follow the first edition, with Taylor indicating in his notes to the movement that he believes the difference to be intentional.

ⓓ Nägeli shows a B-natural on the third sixteenth note of measure 93. All of the referenced editors use B-flat, as shown in Simrock; Hauschild notes the discrepancy.

74

Although no *sf* appears in measure 175 in either Nägeli or Simrock, many editors add the sign on the downbeat in order to render the pattern here analogous to those that follow in measures 177–193. Thus, d'Albert, Bülow, Casella, Köhler, Martienssen, and Schenker add the marking without comment. Arrau, Krebs, and Taylor put it in parenthesis. Only Hauschild, Tovey, and Wallner follow the first edition, Tovey arguing against the addition in his notes.

The LH fingering in measures 175–176 and 183–184 appears in Simrock, but not in Nägeli.

Nägeli shows an erroneous E on beat 2 of measure 183 in the LH. Simrock corrected it.

Sonata No. 18 in E-flat Major

Ludwig van Beethoven (1770–1827)

Op. 31, No. 3

(a) In Simrock the grace notes in measures 11, 18, 19, 101, 102, 147, 154, 155 and 238 are written as small sixteenth notes (♪). Nägeli presents them as eighth notes with a slash through the stem (♪), perhaps suggesting an *acciaccatura*, and thus a more rapid execution. Is it possible that the notation of the grace notes was one of the mistakes in Nägeli that troubled the composer? Taylor apparently thinks so, for in his notes he directs the performer to play the grace note on the beat quickly "but not as a crushed note." Of the referenced editors, seven follow Nägeli's and six follow Simrock's notation.

(b) It should be noted that in both Nägeli and Simrock the grace note in measure 18 is written as F, the note above the main note. All of the referenced editors have deemed this an error, and have changed the note to D to match the grace notes in measures 101 and 154.

(c) All of the referenced editors start the trills in measures 22, 23, 105, and 106 on the main note. Schnabel, Taylor, and Tovey recommend a seven-note figure, including the after-notes (*nachschlag*):

measure 22:

Arrau is content with five notes, and some performers may agree that five notes are more comfortable at tempo.

(d) The dynamic markings in measures 44–45 are presented here as they appear in both Nägeli and Simrock. Several editors, however, have questioned playing the first two quarter notes in the RH *p*. Thus, d'Albert and Schenker add *f* to the RH quarters. Krebs and Schnabel place an *f* in parentheses. Schnabel, apparently conflicted, then adds a small editorial *p* to the same quarter notes and argues for his addition in a footnote. Bülow adds a *p* to the two quarters and the interval of a third in the LH (thus removing the first *f*) and changes the remaining three *f* marks to sforzandi. Casella, Taylor, and Tovey argue in notes for the correctness of the first editions, Casella even suggesting the A in the interval of a third on beat 2 in the LH be redistributed to the RH in order to highlight the sequence of *f*'s (and in so doing renders the two-note slur in the RH very difficult to effect).

(e) Taylor suggests a subtle grouping for the twelve thirty-second notes of 4+5+3. Bülow regroups the notes into two sets of six each and offers a facilitation (questionable in this editor's opinion):

(f) The after-notes (*nachschlag*) are missing for measures 65, 67, and 191 in both Nägeli and Simrock. Eleven of the referenced editors indicate adding them either in notes, by writing them in (sometimes in parentheses), or through fingering suggestions. Inexplicably, Tovey and Wallner (1953) leave them off measure 65. Bülow, Schnabel, and Taylor recommend a seven-note figure starting on the main note and including the after-notes:

measure 65:

Strangely, Schnabel suggests a nine-note figure for the trills on beat 3 of measures 71 and 201. Arrau's fingering possibly suggests a five-note figure, which some performers may find more comfortable.

(g) The dynamic markings for measures 72, 76, and 77 are consistent in both Nägeli and Simrock. However, several editors have targeted this passage for additions. Casella, Köhler, Martienssen, Schenker, and Tovey indicate a crescendo starting in the last eighth note of measure 75. D'Albert starts the crescendo in measure 73. Bülow totally rewrites the dynamics with an array of dynamic and articulation markings. Schnabel, following the scheme in the first editions, adds an editorial *p* in small letters just before the *f* mark in measure 76.

(h) Casella facilitates measures 73 and 74 as follows:

He applies a similar pattern of division to measures 203–204.

(i) Most editors agree that the trills in measures 78 and 209 should start on the main note. Thirty-second notes for the trill work well with a triplet sixteenth for the after-notes (*nachschlag*) in measure 81:

measure 81:

Apply these comments to measures 209–212.

86

(j) Nägeli and Simrock agree in their representations of the trills in measures 115, 123, 125, 127, 128, 129, and 130. The first four trills do not show after-notes (*nachschlagen*); the final three do. It is not as easy to add after-notes in the three measures in which they are missing as it was in earlier examples in this movement (see footnote (f)) because of the ensuing sixteenth-note arpeggiation in measures 124 and 126. Casella argues against adding them in measures 115, 123, and 125. Hauschild, Krebs, Martienssen, Wallner, and this editor simply follow the first editions, thus not adding after-notes in this passage where they are not written. The remaining eight editors indicate using after-notes, d'Albert, Schnabel, and Taylor adding a flat sign to the after-note D at the end of measure 123 in preparation for the downbeat of 124. Whether or not after-notes are used, all six trills should start on the main note, the complete ornament being comprised of seven notes (or five notes, if more comfortable).

(k) Casella offers the following facilitation for measures 124–126 as follows:

① Both Nägeli and Simrock show measure 131 with a **p** on the downbeat. Several editors have deemed this an error, possibly because of the **p** on the last eighth note of the measure, which clearly applies to the RH entrance, thus inferring that the **p** at the beginning of the measure was meant for the LH entrance on the second eighth. Wallner (1953) notes a possible error in a footnote. Hauschild, Martienssen, Schenker, and Wallner (1980) move the **p** so that it clearly applies to the first LH eighth note. Taylor agrees with this decision (as does this editor) in a footnote. D'Albert, Köhler, and Krebs follow the first editions without comment. Arrau, Schnabel, and Tovey follow the first edition and indicate they believe a *subito piano* on the downbeat is correct. Inexcusably, Bülow and Casella omit the first **p** altogether, Bülow adding a **f** to the LH figure.

ⓜ Nägeli and Simrock show **p** on the downbeat of measure 137. This *subito piano* has troubled many editors. Köhler, Krebs, Martienssen, Schenker, Tovey, and Wallner (1953) omit it. The dynamic mark is changed to *poco* **f** in d'Albert, **mf** in Casella, and an editorial **f** in Arrau, Schnabel, and Taylor, the last acknowledging the **p** in the early editions in a footnote. Hauschild, Wallner (1980), and this editor follow the first editions.

(n) The three *f* marks on beats 2 and 3 of measure 168 and on the downbeat of measure 169 appear in Simrock only. Nägeli shows only the last two *f* marks, omitting the one on beat 2 of measure 168. Arrau, Hauschild, Schenker, Wallner, and this editor follow Simrock's text. Taylor follows Nägeli. Krebs, Köhler, Martienssen, Schnabel, and Tovey move the *f* from beat 2 of measure 168, where it applies to the note B-flat, to the downbeat of the measure, Köhler and Schnabel adding *f*'s on beats 2 and 3 of measure 169. D'Albert places *f*'s on beats 1 and 3 of measure 168, omitting the symbol in 169. Bülow substitutes *sf* symbols for beat 3 of measure 168 and the downbeat of measure 169. Casella moves the first *f* to the downbeat of measure 168, substitutes *sf* for beat 3, and shows no symbol in measure 169.

(o) Nägeli and Simrock show *p* on the downbeat of measure 170. Eleven of the referenced editors and this editor move it to the upbeat of the preceding measure. Only Bülow and Casella do not move the mark, but Bülow changes it to *fp* and Casella adds a diminuendo symbol in measure 169.

(q) Both Nägeli and Simrock clearly show the **fp** in measure 208 after the downbeat. Hauschild, Taylor, and Tovey follow the early editions, Taylor remarking on the placement in a footnote. The other ten referenced editors move the symbol to the downbeat, Wallner's footnote deeming the early editions' placement of it an error and pointing to measure 77. This editor follows the first group since both the configuration and articulation of measure 77 is different from that of measure 208.

(r) The LH octave appears without the natural sign in both Nägeli and Simrock, but all editors have regarded this as an omission.

(s) Arrau, Bülow, Schnabel, Taylor, and Tovey add an editorial *p* at the beginning of measure 248.

(t) Nägeli shows *p* for the final two chords of the movement. Simrock shows *f*. Eleven of the referenced editors follow Simrock and end the movement *f*. Hauschild and Wallner (1980) place a *p* symbol in the main text and footnote the difference between the early editions.

SCHERZO
Allegretto vivace

ⓐ In both Nägeli and Simrock, the trill sign is missing in the LH in measure 11. Similarly, the after-notes (*nachschlag*) appear only in the RH of measure 11 and are absent from both hands in measures 30, 118, and 137. All of the referenced editors add the trill sign in measure 11 and the after-notes throughout the movement (except Krebs, who confines his addition to measure 11 alone). The trills all start on the main note. Seven notes, including the after-notes, should work well:

measure 11, RH:

94

(b) The crescendo and diminuendo marks in measures 42–46 and 150–154 are placed in a variety of ways in both Nägeli and Simrock. Most editors adjust these marks so that the diminuendos occur at the harmonic resolutions. This editor concurs in this adjustment.

ⓒ The range of Beethoven's keyboard probably forced the composer to alter the figuration in measure 54. Schenker, Taylor, and Wallner note the limitation, offering no alternative suggestions. Bülow and Schnabel argue against altering Beethoven's solution, a point of view that this editor shares. D'Albert, Casella, Köhler, and Tovey offer the alternative of changing the figuration to match those of measures 51, 53, and 55 an octave higher, Tovey arguing in a note that the composer would have approved.

(d) The dynamic and accentuation in measures 66–107 are represented as they appear in both Nägeli and Simrock. The performer will note that some of the marks that appear in the exposition and recapitulation in conjunction with specific passages are missing. Editors have handled this anomaly in different ways, adding sforzandi and/or crescendo and diminuendo markings to varying degrees consistent with markings used elsewhere in the movement. Some use parentheses or different-sized type to indicate their additions. Others do not. Schnabel takes note of the missing markings. Taylor observes that sforzandi attend the main theme only when it appears in the home key, implying intent. The performer will need to address to what extent markings in the exposition and recapitulation should be imported into the development.

ⓔ Nine of the referenced editors indicate starting the trill in measure 91 on the main note and using after-notes (*nachschlag*).
A five-note turn, including the after-notes, is practical. Only Arrau's fingering suggests a seven-note figure.

98

MENUETTO

Moderato e grazioso

(a) D'Albert, Bülow, and Casella advise playing the turn in measure 9 as thirty-second notes, placed with the fourth eighth note in the LH. Taylor and Tovey prefer a more leisurely ornament:

D'Albert, Bülow, and Casella: Taylor and Tovey:

Schnabel offers both realizations.

(b) There is uncertainty concerning the mark that occurs at the beginning of measures 11, 13, 52, and 54. In both Nägeli and Simrock, the mark is unusually large for an accent and appears between the staves in all four measures. In Nägeli, the marks are close enough to the bar line each time to be interpreted as an accent for the C-flat melody note. Thus, nine of the referenced editors and this editor read the markings as accents. In Simrock, the marking is slightly to the right of the E-flat in each case. This has led Hauschild, Martienssen, Schenker, and Taylor to read the marks as a diminuendo. Taylor acknowledges in a footnote that the markings could be read either way.

(c) All editors start the trill on the main note. Casella, Schenker, Schnabel, Taylor, and this editor recommend not using after-notes (*nachschlag*). A five-note figure works well:

D'Albert, Arrau, and Bülow recommend using after-notes. Schnabel offers the possibility of a seven-note figure, but that seems crowded to this editor.

102

(d) Neither Nägeli nor Simrock show staccato marks in measure 22, but both show staccato in the RH only for the three eighth notes of measure 36. Only Schenker and Wallner reproduce the original text, both without comment. The other eleven editors apply the RH articulation of measure 36 (some in parentheses) to both hands in measures 22 and 36.

Presto con fuoco

(a) Another early edition of this sonata was published as Op. 47 by Clementi, Banger, Hyde, Collard, and Davis (ca. 1804, London). This edition shows the dynamic mark of ***f*** at the opening of this movement.

(b) As in the third movement (see footnote (b) of the *Menuetto*), the markings in both Nägeli and Simrock at measures 3, 5, 9, 11, 176, 178, 182, and 184 are unusually large for accents. Martienssen and Schenker print diminuendo marks. Taylor presents accents in the text, but acknowledges the alternative in a footnote. Bülow solves the problem by using both accents and diminuendo marks!

© Neither Nägeli nor Simrock show a *sf* in the RH in this measure. Of the referenced editors, Bülow, Hauschild, and Wallner add the marking.

106

(d) Eight of the referenced editors indicate starting the trill in measures 63 and 240 on the main note, and five of these suggest using after-notes *(nachschlag)*. A five-note figure works well at tempo:

measure 63:

Schnabel also suggests the possibility of using seven notes. Arrau's fingering suggests starting the trill on the upper note, using six notes, including the after-notes.

108

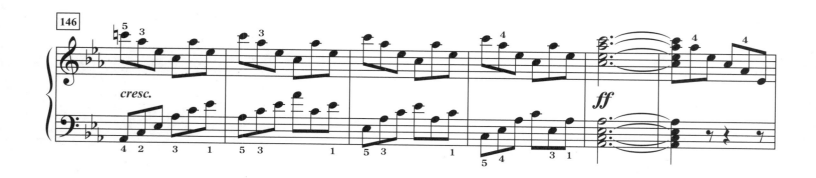

(e) Both Nägeli and Simrock show the following RH notes for measure 165:

All the referenced editors have deemed the change in pattern erroneous.

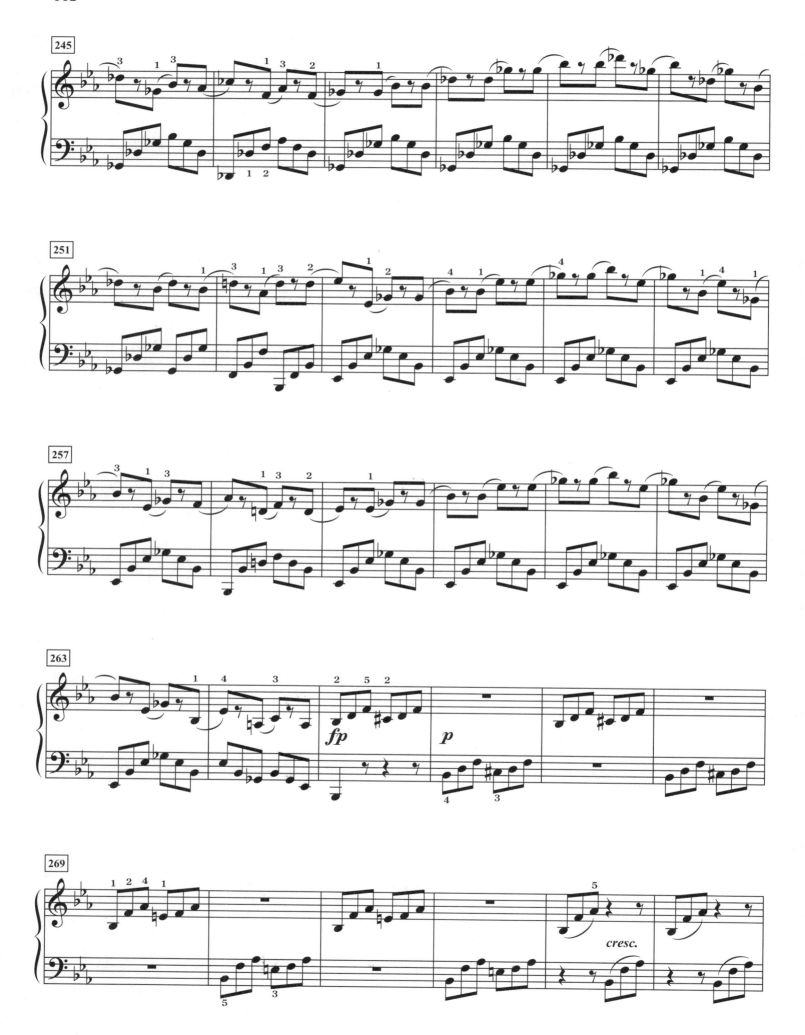

About the Op. 49 Set

The two "easy" sonatas of Op. 49 were likely sketched out in 1797, about the same time the composer was working on the Op. 10 set of sonatas. They were published in January 1805 by the Bureau des arts et d'industrie as *Deux Sonates faciles*. It is believed that the composer had no intention of publishing these works, but that they were intended to be used privately as teaching material. The composer's brother is thought to have sent them to the publisher without Beethoven's knowledge. There must of have been a ready market for the material, however, for by the end of the same year, they were published in Amsterdam and Berlin by Hummel (as Op. 11!) and in Bonn by Simrock (title page reproduced for this edition).

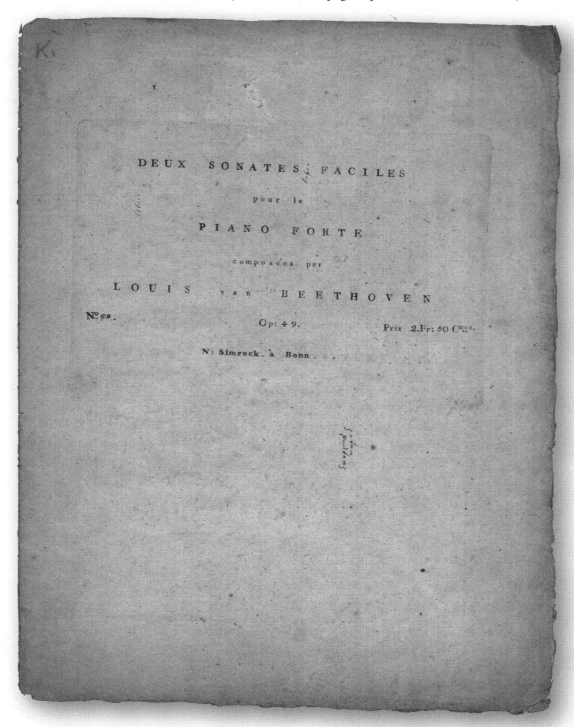

Op. 49 title page from the N. Simrock edition, reproduced by kind permission from the copy in the Austrian National Library, Hoboken Collection, S. H. Beethoven 229

Sonata No. 19 in G Minor (Deux Sonates faciles), Op. 49, No. 1

Autograph/facsimile:	lost
Sketches/loose pages:	none
First edition:	Bureau des arts et d'industrie: Vienna, 1805

The first sonata of the set, marked *Andante*, opens with a compact sonata-allegro movement in G minor. The first theme and second theme are rhythmically related in that they both open with four eighth notes. The second theme area of the exposition (measures 16–33) is traditionally in the relative major (B-flat). A closing figure (measures 29–33) is drawn from the second theme. The development section (upbeat to measure 34–63) opens with the aforementioned four eighth notes, and, after some expansion, quotes the second theme in new keys. The recapitulation (measures 64–110) is regular, presenting second theme material in the home key and extending the closing section to form a short coda (measures 103–110), which comes to rest in the parallel major of the movement (G major), thus preparing the listener for the key of the second movement.

The second *Allegro* movement is called a Rondo by the composer. Its pattern is somewhat unusual: **A B C B A C A** coda. The two **B** sections (measures 20–31 and 68–80) are in G minor, while the **C** sections are presented first in B-flat major (measures 32–67) and then in the home key of G major (measure 103 through the downbeat of 135). The final statement of **A** (upbeat to measure 136–148) is incomplete and incorporates a dialogue between the right and left hands. It leads to a short coda that ends the work (upbeat to measure 149–164).

Sonata No. 20 in G Major (Deux Sonates faciles), Op. 49, No. 2

Autograph/facsimile:	lost
Sketches/loose pages:	none
First edition:	Bureau des arts et d'industrie: Vienna, 1805

The second sonata of the set, like the first, opens with a miniature sonata-allegro movement, marked *Allegro, ma non troppo*. The second theme area of the exposition (upbeat to measure 21–52) is in the expected dominant (D major) and is extended through the use of scalar passage work (measures 36–48). The short development section (measures 53–66) is based mainly on the first theme of the exposition. The recapitulation (measures 67–122) is regular. There is no coda.

The composer's indication of *Tempo di Menuetto* indicates the character of the second movement, although its structure (**A B A C A**) resembles that of a simple rondo. The **A** sections appear each time in the home key of G major (upbeat to measure 1 through the downbeat of 20; upbeat to 48–67; and upbeat to 88–107). The **B** section (with transitions leading to and from it) is presented in the dominant (D major) (upbeat to measure 21–47). The **C** section (upbeat to measure 68–87) starts abruptly, a change in key signature ushering in C major material with a rhythmic figure that is possibly derived from **A**.

Sonata No. 19 in G Minor
(Deux Sonates faciles)

Ludwig van Beethoven (1770–1827)
Op. 49, No. 1

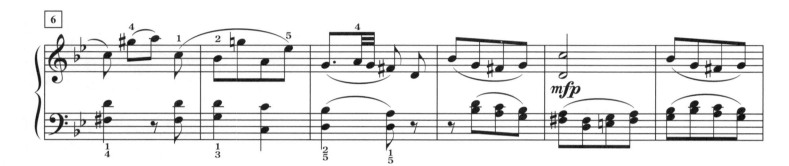

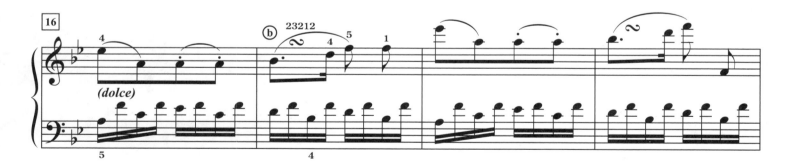

(a) Bülow, Taylor, and Tovey recommend beginning the grace notes in measures 14 and 15 on the beat, simultaneously with the LH. This editor agrees.

(b) D'Albert, Bülow, Casella, Schnabel, Taylor, and this editor recommend the most uncomplicated realization of the turns in measures 17, 19, 21, 22, 25, 81, 83, 85, 86, 88, 89, 90, and 91:

measure 17:

Schnabel and Tovey suggest the following as an alternative:

Schenker's realization:

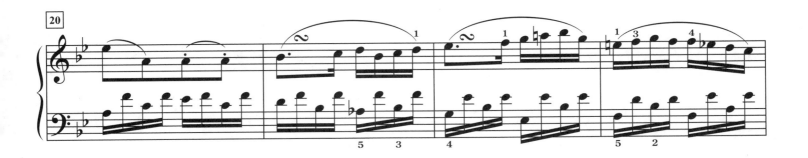

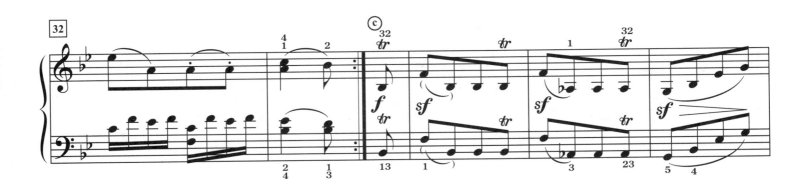

ⓒ The majority of the referenced editors start the trills in measures 33, 34, and 35 on the main note. Arrau, Hauschild, and Wallner indicate fingering that suggests starting on the upper note. Seven of the referenced editors indicate using after-notes (*nachschlag*). Schnabel and Taylor include notes advising against using them. Following is the most frequently encountered realization:

RH upbeat to measure 134: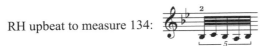

This editor agrees with the group that prefers starting on the upper note, perhaps appropriate given the fact that the two sonatas of Op. 49 date from an earlier period than the opus number suggests.

120

ⓓ The grace notes in measures 43 and 44 appear in the first edition as represented here (♪). Six editors preserve this notation, the others substitute ♪. In either case, play the grace notes very rapidly (as Tovey recommends in a note) before the beat.

122

RONDO

Allegro

ⓐ All the grace notes in this movement are written as small sixteenth notes. Six of the referenced editors substitute ♪ for single grace notes throughout the movement. Bülow, Schnabel, and Taylor indicate on-the-beat execution for the double grace notes in measures 3 and 83. This editor agrees.

ⓑ The first edition shows no articulation in measures 9–11 and 89–91. Hauschild, Krebs, Martienssen, Taylor, Wallner, and this editor follow the first edition. D'Albert, Bülow, Casella, Köhler, Schenker, Schnabel, and Tovey add articulation:

Arrau suggests it editorially and Taylor recommends it in a footnote.

ⓒ The editorial crescendo in measures 20–21 and 24–25 are added here since they appear in an identical passage in measures 68–69 and 72–73. In addition, most editors believe ties in the RH of measures 26 and 74 are missing in the first edition, the rhythm being represented accurately by measures 75 and 76.

(d) D'Albert and Bülow suggest the following for measures 55 and 63:

Casella notates the text as follows:

This editor likes Tovey's ingenious realization, which he states will avoid "stiffness."

Apply these possibilities to measures 126 and 134.

ⓔ The dynamic markings in measures 120 and 122 follow those of the first edition. Only Hauschild and Taylor follow the first edition, Taylor pointing to the fact that the pattern is different from marks in measures 49–50, 51–52, 128–129, and 130–131. The other referenced editors change the marks to conform to the similar passages.

ⓕ The first edition shows the LH in measure 133 to be as follows:

Krebs and Martienssen follow this pattern.

Hauschild, Schnabel, Taylor, and Wallner acknowledge the pattern but deem it erroneous. The remaining referenced editors simply change it to conform to measure 125 without comment.

Sonata No. 20 in G Major
(Deux Sonates faciles)

Ludwig van Beethoven (1770–1827)
Op. 49, No. 2

(a) There are no dynamic markings in the first edition of this sonata except for measures 46 and 86 of the second movement. Only Wallner and Krebs refrain from offering editorial dynamics throughout the sonata. This editor joins Hauschild by including the dynamic markings that appeared in the early Haslinger edition of the work (ca. 1833).

(b) All of the referenced editors whose intention is clear start this trill on the main note in measures 4, 8, and 70. Schnabel and Bülow recommend a seven-note ornament:

measure 4:

For less skilled players, a five-note ornament will suffice:

(c) D'Albert, Bülow, Casella, Schnabel, and Tovey offer the following good realization:

ⓓ Bülow, Schnabel, Taylor, and Tovey recommend playing the grace notes at the beginning of measures 36, 40, 56, 75, 103, and 107 on the beat, simultaneously with the LH.

132

ⓔ The first edition presents the appoggiatura in measure 42 as a small quarter note between the third and fourth quarter notes of the RH. This has led d'Albert, Bülow, Casella, Köhler, Schnabel, and Tovey to interpret the note as a long appoggiatura (♩ ♫). Schenker and Taylor dispute this realization, preferring ♩ ♫. . This editor likes the latter realization.

134

Ⓕ Of the referenced editors who offer advice on executing this
trill, all agree that after-notes (*nachschlag*) should be used.
Seven start on the main note using a seven-note figure:

Arrau prefers a six-note figure starting on the upper note:

Bülow and Tovey allow both.

(a) Casella, Köhler, and Schnabel alter the first edition articulation in measures 28–29 and 32–33 from ♩ ♪ to the easier ♩ ♪. Bülow includes both articulations. Taylor keeps the first edition articulation in the text but states in a note that the easier version may be played.

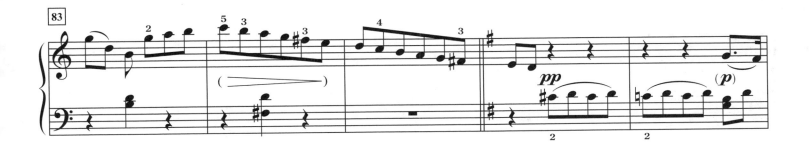

About Op. 53

Op. 53 title page from the first edition, reproduced by kind permission from the copy in the Austrian National Library, Hoboken Collection, S. H. Beethoven 244

Beethoven completed the Op. 53 between May and November of 1803, spending much of this period in the resorts of Baden and Oberdöbling, not far from Vienna. Sketches of the Op. 53 show that the composer was working on the sonata along with the Symphony No. 3, Op. 55 ("Eroica"), and the opera *Fidelio*, Op. 70, especially the overture to it known as *Leonore Overture No. 2*. Sketches for the Op. 53 are particularly interesting for studying the process through which the composer transformed initial thematic fragments into final versions.

The composer offered the Op. 53, along with several other works to Breitkopf & Härtel in a letter dated August 26, 1804. Apparently the offer was not consummated, for the work was published by the Bureau des arts et d'industrie in May of 1805 with the elaborate title, "Grande Sonate pour le Pianoforte, composée et dédiée à Monsieur le Comte de Waldstein, Commandeur de l'ordre Teutonique à Virnsberg et Chambellan de Sa Majesté J. & J. R. A. par Louis van Beethoven, Op. 53."

Count Ferdinand Ernest Gabriel von Waldstein (1762–1823) had been a patron of Beethoven from the time both men resided in Bonn, the Count having been dispatched there from Vienna on a diplomatic mission. It was probably through the influence of the Count that Beethoven was sponsored by the Elector of Bonn, Maximilian Franz (1756–1801) to go to Vienna to study with Haydn. At the time of Beethoven's departure for Vienna, Waldstein wrote in the composer's autograph book, *"May you receive the spirit of Mozart through the hands of Haydn."*

Waldstein's political and financial fortune were depleted by the time the Op. 53 was dedicated to him, for the Count was obsessed with defeating Napoléon Bonaparte (1769–1821) to an extent that he was banished from the Viennese court and spent both his and his wife's fortunes trying to persuade Austria to declare war on Napoléon. Years later, Waldstein died in poverty and disgrace. Exactly how the dedication of this particular sonata became the popular nickname for the work is apparently unknown.

An autograph for the Op. 53 is extant, but there is speculation as to whether or not it was the basis used for the first edition, due to the number of differences between the two sources. Perhaps the engraver's carelessness can account for the differences; on the other hand, scholars have speculated that if, indeed, the engraver of the first edition was working from another manuscript, it may have represented the composer's final editing of the sonata.

Ferdinand Ries (1784–1838), Beethoven's lifelong friend who wrote a biographical sketch of the composer in 1838, reported that the original second movement of the Op. 53 was a much more extended piece, removed from the Op. 53 by the composer after friends suggested it was too long. (Perhaps Ries himself made the suggestion.) The movement appeared separately at the same time as the sonata (WoO 57) and bears the nickname "Andante Favori."

Sonata No. 21 in C Major (Grande Sonate), Op. 53

Autograph/facsimile:	survived
Sketches/loose pages:	yes
First edition:	Bureau des arts et d'industrie: Vienna, 1805

The opening *Allegro con brio* movement of the Op. 53 is cast in a sonata-allegro form of grand dimensions. One of its famous hallmarks is that the opening theme of repeated chords is first stated in the home key (C major) and then abruptly lowered a whole step (to B-flat major at measure 5). There is a return to the opening theme by way of the parallel minor (C minor at measures 12–13), the composer displaying in a few measures a remarkable array of keys. An exciting transition (measures 23–34) leads to a second theme area in the E major, a departure from the expected relationship between first and second themes of sonata-allegro expositions. A chorale-like theme opens this section and is then repeated with an accompaniment of eighth-note triplets (measures 35–49). At this point the triplet figure takes the spotlight and leads to sixteenth-note passage work that culminates in a brilliant E major cadence (measures 50–74). A closing section (measures 74–86) starts in E, but modulates to accommodate the repeat of the exposition or the onset of the development. The development section begins by manipulating the opening theme (measures 92–113), and then moves to develop the triplet eighth-note figure associated with the second theme (measures 113–143). The transition back to the recapitulation builds incredible tension through the use of an ostinato bass figure based on dominant harmony (measure 144 through the downbeat of 158). The recapitulation offers further surprises: a short excursion in the keys of D-flat and E-flat major in the first theme area (measures 171–175); the chorale like portion of the second theme presentation first in A major and A minor before arriving at the home key (measure 198 through the downbeat of 205), and a closing section that modulates unexpectedly to D-flat major (measure 249 through the downbeat of 251). The last-mentioned modulation ushers in a developmental coda of sizeable proportions (measures 251–304), one that develops the opening theme to an exciting climax (measures 251–284); restates the chorale theme (measures 286–296), and ends brilliantly with a final statement of **A** (measures 297–304).

The *Adagio molto* Introduction that leads to the final Rondo is traceable with its own **A B A** form. Its opening rising figure in F major is almost immediately altered to function as an augmented sixth chord, resolving to an E major chord. The **A** section cadences, however, in F major (measure 9), and the **B** section (measures 10–16) is clearly grounded in that key. The return of **A** is partial, the opening figure rising on the dominant of C major, followed by a half-cadence that prepares the way for the final movement (measures 21–28).

The structure of the extended Rondo, marked *Allegretto moderato*, is **A B A C** development **A B** coda. The opening theme is stated two and one-half times in its first two appearances (measures 1–62 and 114–175) and one and one-half times in its return the third time (measures 313–344). The first **B** section (upbeat to measure 63–113) is comprised of two ideas, figuration based on broken chords in C major (measures 63–70) and a vigorous theme in A minor (upbeat to measure 71 through the downbeat of 98), and it concludes with a transition based on the opening idea (measures 98–113). In the later return of **B** (measures 344–402), only the figuration is used but it is extended, leading to an elaborate dominant preparation (measures 378–402). The middle section of the movement (**C**) consists of a new theme in C minor (upbeat to measure 176–220), followed by a development of the opening phrase of the **A** theme (measures 221–250), which becomes fragmented even further (measures 251–312). The final *Prestissimo* coda (measures 403–543) is also based on the **A** theme, its opening idea passing through a myriad of keys and being decorated with technical devises such as glissando octaves and extended trills, all bringing this work to a brilliant close.

Beethoven's autograph of Sonata No. 21 in C Major, *Op. 53, first movement, measures 223–232*

Dedicated to Count Ferdinand von Waldstein

Sonata No. 21 in C Major
(Grande Sonate)

Ludwig van Beethoven (1770–1827)
Op. 53

(a) Both the autograph and the first edition show all grace notes in this movement as small sixteenth notes (♪).
Of the referenced editors, Arrau, Hauschild, Krebs, Schenker, Taylor, and Wallner keep the original notation.
D'Albert, Bülow, Casella, Köhler, Martienssen, Schnabel, and Tovey show ♪ instead. Taylor recommends
playing the notes on the beat, rapidly, but not as crushed notes (*acciaccatura*).

(b) Bülow suggests the fermata should equal an extra whole note, counted in time. Casella objects to the "squareness" of this
recommendation, suggesting instead an extra dotted half note (♩.) or whole note tied to a quarter (𝅗𝅥♩).

146

(c) The autograph shows two decresc. indications in both measures 31 and 194, one for the entrance of each hand. The first edition shows two indications in measure 31, but only one in 194. Of the referenced editors, d'Albert, Köhler, Krebs, Martienssen, and Schenker follow the first edition, repeating the inconsistency. Only Schnabel and Taylor preserve both indications in both places, Taylor pointing to the conceptual importance of having both in a footnote.

148

(d) The autograph and the first edition show cresc. in measure 70, but editorial agreement deems this an error, favoring instead the decresc. indicated in both sources in the parallel passage at measure 233.

(e) Six of the referenced editors and this editor show fingering that suggests starting the trill on the main note. This execution is possible by using sixteenth notes for the trill in coordination with the RH sixteenth notes, with a sixteenth-note triplet at the end to accommodate the after-notes (*nachschlag*). Only Bülow suggests starting on the upper accessory. In Bülow's realization, the ease of executing the after-notes is offset by an intervallic pattern that weakens the dominant sonority, so this editor does not recommend it.

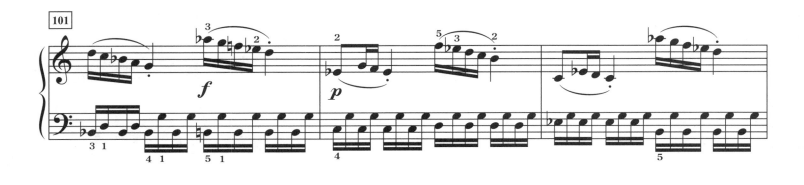

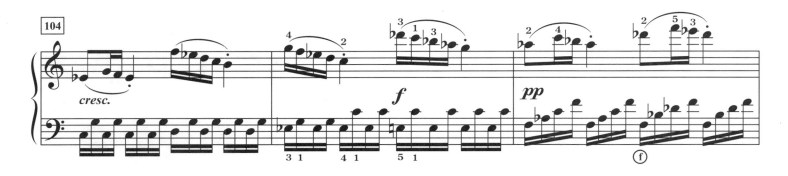

(f) In his edition, Czerny shows the LH of measure 106, beats 3 and 4, as F, A-flat, D-flat, F. Casella speculates Beethoven made this change after the first edition had gone to press. Bülow argues against the change in a footnote. The autograph shows F, B-flat, D-flat, F.

(g) The autograph shows the first two beats of measure 107 as F-flat, G-flat, B-flat, and D-flat. The flat is missing from the F in the first edition. All of the referenced editors except Taylor follow the first edition, Hauschild and Wallner noting the discrepancy in a footnote. Following the first edition rather than the autograph ties in with the theory that another autograph copy was used as the basis for the first edition's engraving and/or that the composer continued to revise his work at each stage of the publication process (see the introductory notes to this sonata). Taylor states that the case for the F-flat is strengthened by the fact that using it would render measure 107 harmonically parallel to measures 109 and 111. Such an argument, however, does not take into account the use of C-natural in the LH figuration of measure 110, where Beethoven could have used C-flat if he had wanted parallel harmonic progressions.

158

(h) The autograph shows the following RH at the opening of measure 233.

The composer then uses repeat symbols (𝄍) for the rest of that measure and measure 234. The engraver of the first edition reproduces this figure with yet another alteration, substituting B for G at the second sixteenth note. Most of the referenced editors simply present these measures with figuration parallel to that in measures 70–71. Schenker, Schnabel, Wallner, and Taylor point to these irregularities, Taylor even deeming the figuration in the autograph "attractive."

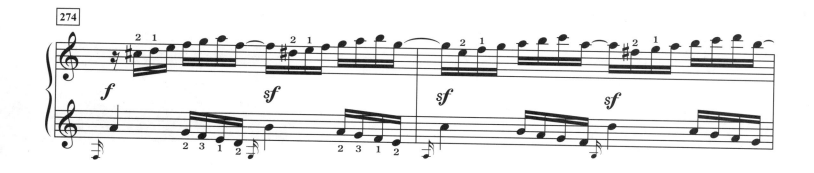

162

INTRODUZIONE
Adagio molto

(a) The grace notes on the downbeats of measures 10 and 12 are written as small thirty-second notes in both the autograph and the first edition. Arrau, Hauschild, Schenker, Wallner, and Taylor preserve this notation. (Krebs may have attempted to do so, but managed only sixteenth notes.) The remaining referenced editors use small eighth notes with a slash through the stem (♪). Taylor and Tovey make a case for playing the grace notes on the beat, notwithstanding the fact that the LH doubling in measure 10 might suggest rapid execution before the beat.

Attacca subito il Rondo

(b) The two B-flats in the LH starting on beat 4 are not tied in either the autograph or the first edition. D'Albert, Bülow, Casella, Köhler, and Tovey add ties. Schnabel and Taylor write footnotes urging repetition of the B-flat.

(c) The grace note on beat 6 in measure 14 is written as a small sixteenth note in both the autograph (where it is barely visible) and the first edition. Arrau, Hauschild, Krebs, Schenker, Wallner, and Taylor preserve this notation. The remainder of the referenced editors substitutes a small eighth note with a slash through the stem (♪).

(a) The autograph shows only *allegretto*. The *moderato* appears in the first edition.

(b) The pedaling throughout this movement comes from both the autograph and the first edition. Beethoven's interest in pedal effects has been evidenced before in the piano sonatas (see footnote (a) for the first movement of the Op. 27, No. 2, Volume II of this edition; and footnote (d) for the first movement of the Op. 31, No. 2 in this volume). That Beethoven wanted a coloristic sonority with some degree of blurring seems certain. However, achieving whatever effect the composer wanted on today's instruments that are more resonant is problematic for many. Of the referenced editors, Köhler and Bülow change the original pedaling to achieve harmonic clarity. Schenker, Taylor, and Tovey write notes suggesting unspecified patterns of "half-pedaling" (i.e., half-damping), Taylor and Tovey indicating that using the sostenuto (middle) pedal when it is available might be helpful. Casella and Schnabel in notes extol the originality of the composer's sonic conception and insist that the performer follow the original pedaling. The remaining editors simply reproduce the original pedaling without comment. This editors sides with those who attempt to follow Beethoven's markings exactly, which is possible on most pianos with careful attention to touch, balance, and exact pedal releases.

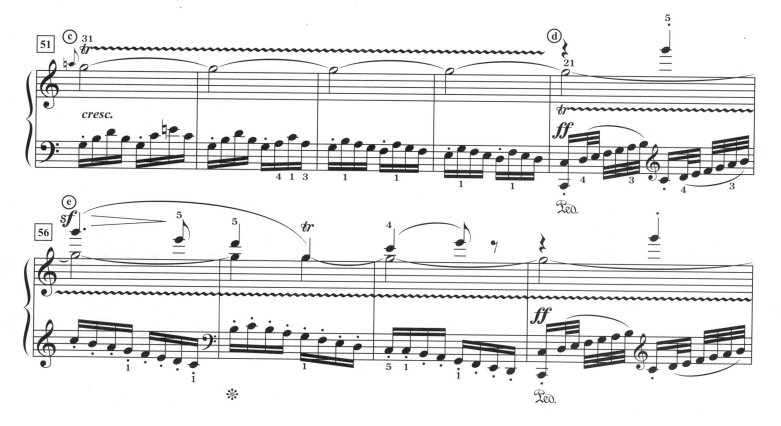

(c) The RH grace note raises questions that have far-reaching effects in this movement. Did the composer write the grace note to ensure starting on the upper accessory in an age when doing so was changing? Or is the grace note meant to be played rapidly before the downbeat to ensure starting the downbeat with the main note? If the performer uses a measured trill (sextuplets are often suggested), then downbeats of ensuing measures will begin with whichever note was used to start the trill (see footnote (d)).

(d) At the end of the autograph Beethoven wrote out two possible realizations of measure 285 (see footnote (1)). Some editors have used these composer's examples as the basis for approaching all the passages in this movement where one hand is required to both trill and play the main theme (e.g., measures 55–61, 168–174, 337–343, and 485–506). This approach raises problems: the frequent stretch of the interval of a seventh at the onset of the melody (e.g., see beat 2 of measure 55), and the fact that at one point a G in the melody forms the interval of a major second with the trill (e.g., see beat 2 of measure 57). Arrau, Hauschild, Köhler, and Wallner do not address this issue. Instead, they suggest fingering that is in keeping with starting beats with the upper note, except for places where the aforementioned interval of a second would occur. In those spots, the starting note shifts so that it coincides with the melodic G. Schenker, Schnabel, Tovey, and Taylor provide notes that suggest strict adherence to Beethoven's model, although Taylor allows the so-called "false trill" as a possibility. Bülow simply rewrites the passages using the "false trill," a technique that J. S. Bach had exploited in Variation 28 of the "Goldberg" Variations (S. 988) and both Czerny and Hummel had illustrated in piano methods.

D'Albert, Casella, Martienssen, and this editor allow for shifting the trill so that the melodic notes occur with the main note of the trill. William S. Newman agrees with allowing the execution of these passages to follow patterns that are more pianistic, suggesting that Beethoven may have lost touch with the physical aspect of playing the piano due to his increasing deafness. (*Beethoven on Beethoven: Playing His Piano Music His Way*; W. W. Norton, New York, 1988, p. 216.) This editor uses the following arrangement:

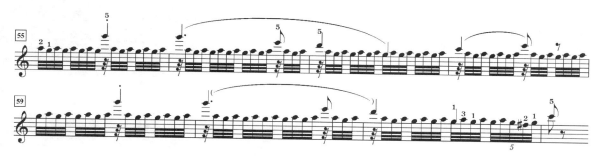

(e) The autograph shows *sf* on the downbeats of measures 56, 169, 173, 338, and 342. (This mark is missing from measure 60, probably an oversight.) The first edition shows none of these sforzandi. Krebs, Schenker, and Schnabel follow the first edition. All of the other referenced editors either point out this discrepancy in a footnote or add the sforzandi into the text. A second issue is that the first edition shows no slurring in measures 60–61, 173–174, or 341–342. Slurring is missing in measures 60–61 of the autograph as well. Most editors, including this one, believe these parallel passages should be consistent and add slurs accordingly. Only Krebs and Schenker demur, following instead the first edition.

(f) Measures 101, 105, 113 as well as a later group, 395, 397, and 399, employ multiple eighth and quarter rests in lieu of whole rests. As this notation exists in both the autograph and the first edition, it is believed that the composer used the device to show exactly where to release the damper pedal. Seven of the referenced editors adopt this multi-rest notation, with Schenker, Schnabel, Taylor, and Wallner pointing out the exactness in notating the pedal releases in footnotes. Krebs and Tovey use less exact notation, the latter suggesting unclearly some kind of pedal adjustment in measures 100 and 104 to alleviate the harmonic blur. D'Albert, Bülow, Casella, and Köhler inexcusably alter the composer's pedaling to ensure harmonic clarity.

(g) The pedaling for measures 235 through the downbeat of measure 239 offers another example of the composer's mixing tonic and dominant harmonies. As expected, Köhler and Bülow change the pedaling so that each harmony is clear. Martienssen and Casella, heretofore having often honored Beethoven's pedaling, also opt for clarity here. Taylor suggests in a note that these measures may need "modification" with regard to pedaling.

(h) Beethoven's long pedal marking sustaining dominant harmony from measure 295 to beat 2 of measure 312 is acceptable to all but two of the referenced editors. The A-flat and G octaves in the LH in measure 305–308 bother Casella and Taylor, who suggest a modification because of the sonority of today's piano. Tovey, on the other hand, encourages the performer to let the A-flat "growl mysteriously" against the G.

(i) From measures 314–327, the first edition fails to reproduce several of the sforzandi and dynamic marks evident in the autograph. This text shows the autograph version. Of special note are the parallel dynamic patterns of measures 321–323 and 325–327, wherein measures 321 and 325 start fortissimo, leading to a piano in measures 323 and 327. A decrescendo mark is found in measure 322, but is missing from 326. The composer's dynamic scheme seems clear in the autograph, but of the referenced editors only Arrau, Hauschild, Taylor, and Wallner take note of it. The remaining editors apply a pianissimo at measure 321.

176

178

attacca subito il Prestissimo

179

(j) The fingering in measures 465 and 467 appears in both the autograph and the first edition. It is generally agreed that the fingering indicates octave glissandi, a feat made easier on Beethoven's piano by its light action and more shallow key dip. Glissandi are still possible on modern day instruments for performers with sizeable hands. Wrist octaves are not possible at tempo, and none of the editors suggests slowing to accommodate them. D'Albert, Bülow, Casella, Martienssen, Schenker, and Schnabel each offer their arrangement for splitting the octaves between the hands. Splitting is fairly easy to achieve in measures 465–466 and 469–470 leaving out a note or two where the LH must execute large skips:

Measures 467–468 and 471–472 are more problematic because of the whole and half notes in the RH. Bülow, Casella, Martienssen, and Schenker resort to single notes in the LH (using lower octave notes). Schnabel splits the octaves between two hands indicating pedaling to sustain the RH chords, resulting in considerable blurring. D'Albert suggests an arrangement that this editor finds impractical at tempo:

(k) All editors agree that this trill should begin on the main note.

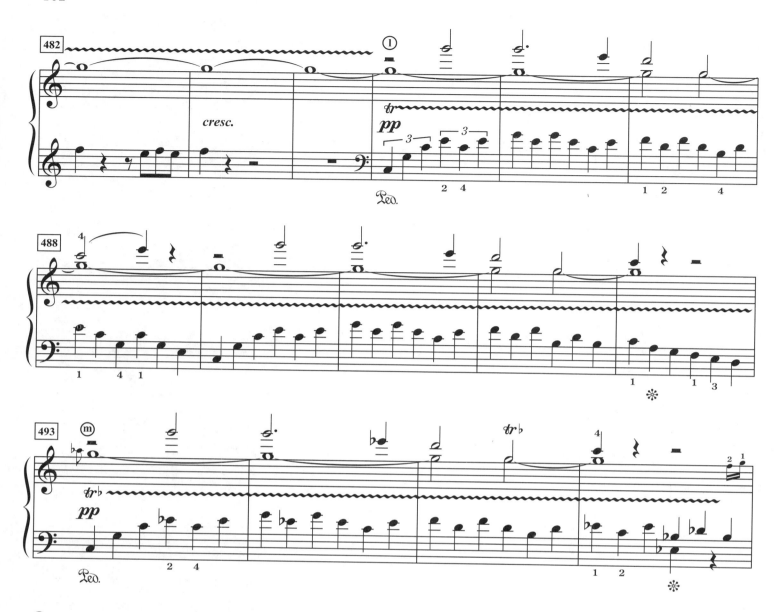

① Beethoven's guidance for this passage was discussed in footnote ⓓ. Since the composer wrote his realizations in the context of this passage, his examples are reproduced here:

or easier:

The composer's fragments, however, do not show how to proceed when the trill changes pitch or when after-notes (*nachschlag*) are involved. Several of the referenced editors attempt to clarify these issues by providing more nearly complete realizations of measures 485–507.

Bülow uses the "false trill" in eighth notes throughout maintaining upper accessories (see footnote ⓓ). Schenker and Schnabel keep the trill unbroken with the same approach, Schenker adding extra notes to accommodate *nachschlag* and Schnabel simply not including them. Schnabel suggests the possibility of using normal sixteenth notes (not sextuplets), a rhythmic arrangement this editor finds useful at tempo, notwithstanding the polyrhythm that develops (three against four) with the LH.

ⓜ In measure 493, the interval between A-flat and the G a major seventh above it results in a difficult stretch. This editor suggests playing the A-flat grace before the beat, thus shifting the trill to the main note at this point. This arrangement works well to accommodate the *nachschlag* at the end of measure 496, the octave in measure 497, the unison in measure 499, as well as the *nachschlag* in measure 500 (if they are used). In measure 501, the downbeat falls on the main notes and the D-flat grace note is before beat 2. Casella, incidentally, suggests much of this arrangement in a footnote.

(n)   Neither the autograph nor the first edition show after-notes (*nachschlag*) here. D'Albert, Arrau, Bülow, Casella, Köhler, and Schnabel use them, however.

(o)   Whatever adjustments may have been made in the preceding measures, editors advise that the grace notes in measures 507 and 511 should be on the beat and strong. This editor agrees.

(p)   D'Albert, Bülow, Casella, Schenker, Schnabel, and Tovey offer one or both of the following facilitations:

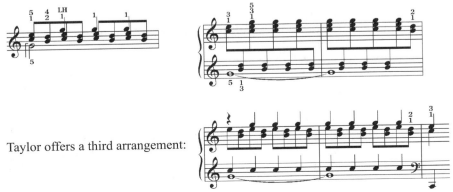

Taylor offers a third arrangement:

184

Ⓠ Neither the autograph nor the first edition close this pedal indication.

About Op. 54

Op. 54 title page from the first edition, reproduced by kind permission from the copy in the Austrian National Library, Hoboken Collection, S. H. Beethoven 250

As with the Op. 53, the Op. 54 is thought to have been offered to Breitkopf & Härtel for publication in a letter dated August 26, 1804. Apparently, the package of compositions was delayed in being sent, so it was not until in a letter dated April 18, 1805, that Beethoven attempted to negotiate the terms for several works in the publisher's possession. By that time, the composer insisted that the two sonatas be published within two months and complained that further delay would harm his reputation. Details of what went wrong with Breitkopf & Härtel are not known, but Op. 54 was not actually published until 1806 by the Bureau des arts et d'industrie. The work bears no dedication.

Perhaps because of its unusual structure, the Op. 54 received a poor review by an unidentified writer in the *Allgemeine musikalische Zeitung*,[34] the work being cited for its "ineffectual peculiarities." Subsequently, the sonata has had its champions, for Donald Francis Tovey (1875–1940) in the notes for his edition finds the work "unique and subtle."

Sonata No. 22 in F Major, Op. 54

Autograph/facsimile: lost
Sketches/loose pages: yes
First edition: Bureau des arts et d'industrie: Vienna, 1806

The Op. 54, marked *In Tempo d'un Menuetto*, opens with a movement that alternates a dignified minuet style with vigorous octaves in an **A B A B A** pattern. Each **A** section is in F major (upbeat to measure 1–24; upbeat to 71–93; and upbeat to 106–136), each appearance of **A** being graced with more elaborate figural decoration and the final one leading to a short cadenza (measures 132–136). The two **B** sections (upbeat to measure 25–69 and upbeat to 94–105) provide contrast, both with regard to key and texture, the first more-extended one moving through C major and A-flat major, and the second remaining in the home key. A short coda based on **A** (upbeat to measure 137–154) brings this simple, but elegant movement to its close.

The structure of the *Allegretto* second movement of the Op. 54 is akin to that of the final movement of Op. 10, No. 2. The movement is based on a perpetually moving idea in sixteenth notes, which offers little thematic contrast. However, within this framework one can discern a reference to the sonata-allegro pattern. The opening exposition section (measures 1–20) modulates to the dominant (C major) and is marked to be repeated. The second section, also marked to be repeated (measures 24–164), develops the main idea, taking it through several keys, and recapitulates it in the home key with some variation (measures 116–164). A coda, marked *Più allegro* (measures 165–191), makes use of the main theme yet once more and brings this movement to a vigorous conclusion with a series of syncopated *sfozandi*.

[34] *Allgemeine musikalische Zeitung* VIII (1805–06), pp. 639–40.

Sonata No. 22 in F Major

Ludwig van Beethoven (1770–1827)
Op. 54

ⓐ The first edition shows several small inconsistencies in the RH slurring of measures 12–16, 20–24, and 81–85. The LH slurring, on the contrary, is the same in all places. The RH slurring presented here is that adopted by most critical editors, all having deemed the shorter groupings that appear randomly as engraving errors.

ⓑ The ornamentation in measures 16, 18, 20, 24, 85, and 113 is cause for disagreement among the referenced editors. The first question is whether the trill symbol in measures 16 and 85 results in different ornamentation from that indicated by the mordent-turn combination used in the other measures. Martienssen, Schnabel, Taylor, and Tovey suggest trills without after-notes (*nachschlag*) in measures 16 and 85. Martienssen and Tovey start on the main note, Taylor and this editor on the upper note, and Schnabel gives examples of both.

measure 16:

C.P.E. Bach designates the combination of a mordent and turn as a "trilled turn," realized as follows:

measure 18, beat 3: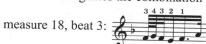

Only Casella, Schnabel, Taylor, and this editor suggest this realization; however, Schnabel also allows an easier version that resembles the models below. The other referenced editors who deal with these ornaments are d'Albert, Bülow, Köhler, and Schenker. They make no distinction between the symbols, with Köhler substituting the turn sign in all of these measures. Their solutions in all cases are one of the following two examples:

measure 18, beat 3:

ⓒ Dynamic indications are missing in measures 17 and 21. Most editors add the crescendo and diminuendo markings in 17 to match those of measures 9–10, 78–79, and 80–81, as well as the cresc. in 21 to match the one in measure 13.

188

(d) The first edition shows no *sf* in measures 40 and 41, unlike measures 26 and 27. D'Albert is the only referenced editor who adds them, as well as others in this passage. Schnabel, Tovey, and Taylor point to this inconsistency in notes, Schnabel and Tovey are hesitant to add them and Taylor suggests that they probably should be added.

(e) The first edition shows *sf* only on beat 2 of measure 46 and the downbeat of measure 47. All of the referenced editors add them in a pattern that matches that used in measures 30–33.

(f) The first edition shows beat 2 in the RH of measure 49 as follows:

Eight of the referenced editors change the octaves to sixths, Casella and Taylor deeming the octaves an error in notes. Five of the editors keep the octaves, Schnabel and Wallner providing notes that question their accuracy.

(g) The figure of a grace note followed by four sixteenth notes is introduced here and used periodically throughout the rest of this movement. This first edition represents all these grace notes as small eighth notes with unadorned stems. Only Arrau, Hauschild, Krebs, Taylor, and Wallner use this notation. The rest of the referenced editors add a slash to the stems of the grace notes. A footnote of Schnabel suggests rapid execution before the beat. Bülow, on the other hand, recommends applying C.P.E. Bach's principle, thus playing them longer and on the beat. This editor prefers playing the grace notes on the beat, but very fast. On-the-beat execution will result in playing the grace note with the lowermost voice in measures 76 and 112, as well as with the alto voice in measures 93, 121, 141, and 142.

(h) The first edition shows the crescendo-decrescendo "hairpins" peaking at beat 3 of measures 78 and 80 rather than the downbeat of 79 and 81. Only Hauschild and Taylor preserve this pattern, Taylor suggesting in a note that it might be an intentional variation. All of the other referenced editors adjust the dynamic markings to conform to those in measures 9–12.

191

① The **p** indication is from the first edition. Tovey questions its accuracy. Bülow omits it. D'Albert and Schenker add a cresc. indication to measure 101. Arrau, Casella, Schnabel, and Taylor indicate in some form *subito* changes for the **p** in measure 101 and the **ff** in measure 102.

j D'Albert, Casella, Schnabel, and Tovey offer realization of this series of trills. They all agree on the following:

k Taylor calls for a full eighth-note appoggiatura, a gesture this editor finds attractive. Schenker implies a similar effect by suggesting to play this appoggiatura with the LH, as well as those on the downbeat of measures 134 and 135.

l The first edition shows the appoggiatura on the downbeat of measure 134 as a small quarter note. Of the referenced editors, only Taylor acknowledges this notation, deeming it an error. This editor finds it plausible. If one were to treat it as a long appoggiatura, the RH trill would then start on beat 2 of the measure, simultaneously with the LH chord.

(m) None of the trills in this movement show wavy lines to indicate how long the trill should extend. This becomes an issue only in measures 133, 134, and 135. Editors agree that the trills in measures 133 and 134 should flow into their respective after-notes (*nachschlagen*). The trill that begins in measure 135 has no such after-notes. Schnabel and Taylor suggest that the trill should stop on the downbeat of measure 136. D'Albert, Bülow, Casella, Schenker, and Tovey would have the trill flow right into the sextuplet on beat 2 of measure 136.

(n) The fermata sign over the triplet eighth note figure has been the cause of controversy. Köhler, Martienssen, and Schenker omit it entirely. D'Albert, Bülow, Casella, Krebs, and Schnabel apply it to the B-natural. Arrau, Hauschild, Taylor, Tovey, and Wallner show an elongated fermata extending over all three notes of the triplet, an unconventional symbol that would suggest allotting extended time to all three notes. Careful scrutiny of the first edition's engraving, however, shows that the fermata sign over the triplet is the same size as those over the C on beat 1 of the measure and the E-natural, the last of the four sixteenth notes that follow the triplet. It is true that all three fermata signs are somewhat longer than those used today, and the one over the triplet tends to spill over toward the first and third notes. Despite that observation, there is no evidence to support the use of an unconventional elongated fermata. Thus, this editor believes the fermata applies only to the B-natural.

194

(a) Of the referenced editors who deal with the LH trill in measure 21, all start on the main note, but five suggest using after-notes (*nachschlag*) and four recommend not using them. Bülow in a footnote leaves it to the performer's discretion. This editor recommends the following realization:

ⓑ The lower note of the LH octave is missing in the first edition in measures 42–44, a limitation due to the compass of most pianos in Beethoven's time. Most of the referenced editors (as well as this editor) allow adding the lower notes of these octaves since, unlike other instances, the composer did not rewrite any passagework to accommodate such limitations. Arrau, Krebs, Martienssen, and Schnabel indicate single bass notes.

© The first edition shows D-naturals in the RH on the sixteenth-note pattern beginning on beat 2 of measure 71. Bülow, Köhler, and Schenker indicate D-flats. Martienssen, Taylor, and Wallner state either pitch might be appropriate. The remaining referenced editors follow the first edition.

(d) Of the referenced editors who offer advice on this trill, all agree it starts on the main note. D'Albert, Köhler, Martienssen, Schenker, and Taylor suggest after-notes (*nachschlag*) at the end of measure 162. Casella and Schnabel advise against using them. Bülow suggests after-notes when taking the repeat, but not when moving into the coda. D'Albert, Arrau, Bülow, Casella, and Schnabel suggest a small breath before starting the first ending, often commenting on either the subito *pp* and/or the key shift to A major.

ⓔ Measure 185 is in dispute. The first edition shows the RH as represented in the text above. Nine of the referenced editors follow the first edition. Bülow, Casella, Hauschild, and Schenker alter the pattern as follows:

Thus, they deem the first edition in error and point to the rhythmic pattern of *sf* markings in the LH of measures 187–190. In notes Taylor, Tovey, and Wallner also allow for a possible error. Schnabel's footnote favors following the first edition.

About the Op. 57

Beethoven's student Carl Czerny (1791–1857) reported that the composer considered the Op. 57 his *"greatest sonata, up to the period when he composed the Op. 106."*[35] Beethoven began writing the work in the summer of 1804 and probably continued for about two years, a period during which the composer was engaged in writing a number of significant works, including the opera *Fidelio*; Piano Concerto No. 4, Op. 58; the "Rasumovsky" Quartets, Op. 59; the Symphony No. 4, Op. 60; and the Concerto for Violin, Op. 61.

Op. 57 title page from the first edition, reproduced by kind permission from the copy in the Austrian National Library, Hoboken Collection, S. H. Beethoven 259

Thought to be one of three piano sonatas offered to the publisher Breitkopf & Härtel in a letter dated April 18, 1805, the Op. 57 was actually published in Vienna, Austria, by the Bureau des arts et d'industrie in February of 1807. It was published in a four-hand version in Hamburg in 1838 by Cranz under the title *Sonata appassionata*. This seems to be the first use of the designation that became the work's famous nickname. The autograph of the Op. 57 is extant, it having been a gift in 1807 from the composer to the pianist Marie Kiene Bigot de Morogues (1786–1920), who with her husband moved to Paris in 1809 where Mendelssohn studied with her in 1816. Marie gave the autograph to the Paris Conservatoire de Musique in 1889.

The Op. 57 is dedicated to the Count Franz Brunsvik (1777–1849). The Count was a close personal friend of Beethoven, an excellent violoncellist, and his wife, Sidonie Justh (1801–1866), a fine pianist. Beethoven also dedicated the Piano Fantasia, Op. 77, to the Count. Moreover, Beethoven was close to the Count's two sisters, who had piano lessons with him in 1799. Therese, to whom Beethoven dedicated the Op. 78, never married. Josephine was the recipient of several amorous letters from the composer after the death of her first husband, Count Joseph Deym, but she remarried Baron Christoph von Stackelberg in 1810. Josephine was one of several women considered by scholars as possibly the "Immortal Beloved" of Beethoven's famous love letter of July, 6 and 7, 1812.

Sonata No. 23 in F Minor, Op. 57

Autograph/facsimile: survived
Sketches/loose pages: yes
First edition: Bureau des arts et d'industrie: Vienna, 1807

The first movement of the Op. 57, marked *Allegro assai*, opens with one of Beethoven's most famous thematic statements: a dark outlining of an F minor triad at the double octave with a half cadence that is repeated immediately a half-step higher in G-flat major (upbeat to measure 1–8). The conflict implied by the half-step relationship is mirrored in the bass motive that appears in measure 10. Thus the composer sets a mood of tension for this extended movement in sonata-allegro form. A transition theme sustains this tension through the use of a repeated-note accompaniment (measures 24–34). The second theme area of the exposition begins traditionally in the relative major (A-flat) of the movement's minor key with a theme that is rhythmically related to the opening theme (upbeat to measure 36–41). A series of trills leads to a turbulent section in A-flat minor, the key that remains constant through the rest of the exposition (measures 51–65). The exposition flows seamlessly into the development with no repeat. The development section itself makes use of first theme material in its opening section (upbeat to measure 66–92), touches briefly on the transition material (measure 93 through the downbeat of 109), and turns to the second theme (upbeat to measure 110–122). A cadenza-like transition (measure 123 through the downbeat of 134) dramatically leads back to the recapitulation, where the opening material is

---

[35] Carl Czerny, *On the Proper Performance of All of Beethoven's Works for the Piano*, ed. Paul Badura-Skoda (Vienna: Universal Editions, 1970), p. 58.

restated over a repeated-note bass (upbeat to measure 136–150). The second theme is regular, the opening theme being presented in the parallel major (F major) and progressing back to the parallel minor, closing in the home key (upbeat to measure 175–204). The coda (upbeat to measure 205–262) is both extended and developmental. It first works with both the first theme (upbeat to measure 205–210) and the second theme (upbeat to measure 211–217). Then the cadenza-like transition material from the development is borrowed and extended to create a monumental, arching climax (measures 218–238). A closing *Più allegro* follows, presenting once more both second and first themes (upbeat to measure 239–262). The movement ends quietly.

The *Andante con moto* in D-flat major presents a formal two-part theme (each part marked to be repeated) followed by three variations. The variations make use of the so-called "rhythmic crescendo," a procedure of writing increasingly smaller note values for each variation so that each seems to move faster. In the third variation the repeats are written out in order to place thematic material alternately in each hand (upbeat to measure 54–85). The movement closes with a (slightly varied) restatement of the original theme (measures 86–102), but its final cadence presents a surprising diminished seventh harmony, marked first *pp* and then *ff*, as a link to the final movement.

The final *Allegro, ma non troppo* vies with the opening movement in dramatic intensity. It is cast in a sonata-allegro structure with a coda, unusual in that the composer indicates no repeat for the exposition, but directs that the development and recapitulation be repeated. A short introduction (measures 1–19) reiterates the diminished-seventh sonority from the final chords of the second movement and spirals downward to the opening theme of the exposition. The tension between F minor and G-flat major noted in the first movement is also present here in statements of the opening theme (measures 20–28). The exposition makes use of sixteenth-note patterns constantly, so that it gives the impression of being monothematic. A second idea appears (upbeat to measure 29 through the downbeat of 64) but remains in the home key. By the time the modulation to the dominant minor takes place, the exposition is almost over, closing with yet another reiteration of the opening theme (measures 76–117). The development section focuses initially on the main theme, but introduces a new theme, possibly derived from the rhythmic vitality of the second idea in the exposition (measure 142 through the downbeat of 158). A suspenseful transition based again on the opening theme leads to the recapitulation (measures 158–211). The recapitulation (measures 212–315) is regular, ending this time in the tonic minor. The coda (marked *Presto*) (measures 316–371) opens with two short sections of driving chords, each marked to be repeated, followed by a final reiteration of the opening theme, all expertly devised by the composer to bring the work to a compelling, dramatic conclusion.

Beethoven's autograph of Sonata No. 23 in F Minor, *Op. 57, first movement, measures 1–11*

Dedicated to the Count Franz Brunsvik

Sonata No. 23 in F Minor

Ludwig van Beethoven (1770–1827)

Op. 57

ⓐ Slurring for this figure is sporadic in both the autograph and the first edition. When it appears, it is represented as ♪⁀♪♪ . In addition, slurs over the group of three sixteenth notes are often missing.

ⓑ The motivic figure in measure 3 appears throughout this movement, the trill sometimes being preceded by a small grace note, at other times not. Fortunately, the autograph and the first edition correspond as to the notation of these figures. The presence or absence of the grace note has led to a variety of interpretations. Of the referenced editors, Bülow, Casella, Martienssen, Schenker, Schnabel, Tovey, and Taylor provide either notes or realizations that represent his individual point of view, and the views often conflict. In those measures where the lower grace note is present there is a fair amount of agreement with starting the first note on the beat. Only Martienssen wrote it as a grace note before the beat. Moreover, Martienssen, Schnabel, and Taylor show realizations in which the last three sixteenth notes in the measure are to be played in time rather than incorporated into the trill as after-notes (*nachshclag*), and Taylor writes a note stressing such rhythmic accuracy. The following examples are representative of these realizations:

measure 3, beat 7:   or:

This concept can be applied to measures 3, 7, 9, 23, 69, 144, and 146. For measures without a grace note, see footnote ⓒ.

ⓒ The trills in the following measures are presented in both the autograph and the first edition without a grace note before the trill: 11, 21, 71, 73, 76, 138, 142, 156, 158, 160, and 162. A summary of the realizations of the referenced editors who address these trills through comments and/or fingering follows: Arrau, Bülow, Hauschild, Köhler, and Wallner begin these trills on the beat with the upper accessory:

measure 11, beat 7:   measure 21, beat 7:

This editor agrees with this group. Martienssen and Schenker recommend beginning on the upper notes before the beat. Schnabel, although acknowledging the performance practice of using the upper note, prefers to add a lower grace note, thus rendering all of the trills in this movement like the one in measure 3 (see footnote ⓑ). Casella, Tovey, and Taylor believe that one may add a lower grace note to measure 11 inasmuch as its counterpart in the recapitulation shows one (measure 146), although the LH is quite different. Tovey points to the fact that in most cases the lower grace note is omitted where the RH is written in double (or triple) notes (measures 21, 71, 73, 76, 138, 142, 156, and 162). The exceptions are measures 11, and measures 160 and 162. Tovey recommends that all measures except measure 11 be played with trills starting on the upper note. Taylor draws the conclusion that in the absence of a grace note, all trills should start on the main note; then he waffles by adding that one might well add a lower grace note to any of the trills in this movement. Casella adds his own pattern of either upper or lower grace notes throughout the movement, noting that all grace notes should start on the beat.

(d) For the record, it should be noted that d'Albert, Bülow, and Casella offer facilitations of measures 14 and 15. Schenker cautions against using them. This editor agrees with Schenker.

(e) Casella and Köhler facilitate measures 20, 22, 155, 157, and 159 by taking the first chord in each measure with the LH. The remaining referenced editors leave the downbeats to the RH, probably because the presentation in both the autograph and the first edition suggest such. Schnabel writes a note insisting the RH play these downbeats.

(f) Two schools of thought exist among the referenced editors regarding the fingering of the repeated notes in measures 24–34, 93–104, 134–150, and 163–173. D'Albert, Bülow, Casella, Schnabel, and Taylor use the same finger on repeated notes rather than changing fingers. This editor agrees with the belief that using the same finger on repeated notes works acceptably at the tempo of this movement and helps keep LH articulation from overshadowing the RH. The remaining referenced editors offer a variety of changing finger patterns, Schnabel offering one of these as an alternative. Schenker (i.e., Edwin Ratz) suggests mostly alternating between two fingers, most often between the thumb and the index finger.

(g) Schenker and Schnabel show realizations that place the grace notes on the beat, and Casella insists in a note that all grace notes before trills should be played on the beat in this movement. After-notes (*nachschlag*) should be used in measures 44–46 and 183–185 only where indicated. Several editors offer facilitations for the skips. Bülow, Casella, and Köhler suggest playing measures 45 and 184 with the LH, but such facilitation places the LH in an awkwardly high range for trilling. Schenker suggests taking the opening grace notes in measures 45–46 and 184–185 with the LH. D'Albert and Taylor take both the opening grace notes and the after-notes of measures 45 and 184 with the LH, a solution that seems most effective to this editor, providing one subscribes to such facilitations at all. The remaining referenced editors do not.

(h) The autograph and the first edition show E-naturals in measure 53, F-flats not appearing until measure 54. Most editors change the E-naturals to F-flats in measure 53.

208

① Casella, Taylor, and Tovey suggest playing the first C-flat with the LH, thereby eliminating a position change in the RH.

212

ⓙ The pedal indication from measure 123 to the downbeat of measure 132 is in both the autograph and the first edition.

(k) Although the grace note is missing in measure 183 (see measure 44) in both the autograph and the first edition, Arrau, Casella, Hauschild, Schnabel, and Wallner add the F-sharp editorially. Taylor cautiously suggests the possibility of such an addition. D'Albert and Bülow add an A-flat grace note. Schenker's footnote implies not adding the grace note, and Tovey is insistent that the trill start on G. See footnote (g) for possible facilitations in measures 184–185.

① The pedaling in measures 218 through the middle of measure 237 is in both the autograph and the first edition. Especially clear in the autograph are the points of precise release.

Ⓜ Facilitation by dividing the passagework between the RH and LH in measures 227–235 is offered by ten of the referenced editors. Only Arrau and Wallner offer fingering that suggests playing the sweeping arpeggios with only the RH. Schnabel and Schenker express reservation about such facilitations in notes, but then turn around and offer them. There are many patterns of such facilitations. The main body of the text offers one such arrangement in parenthesis as an alternative.

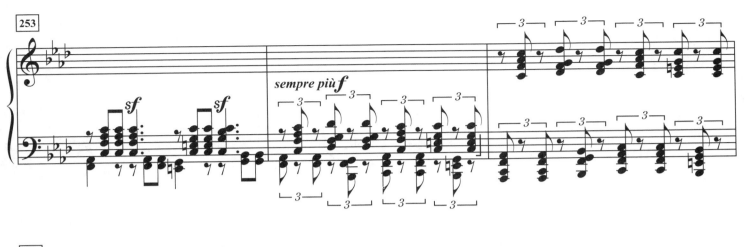

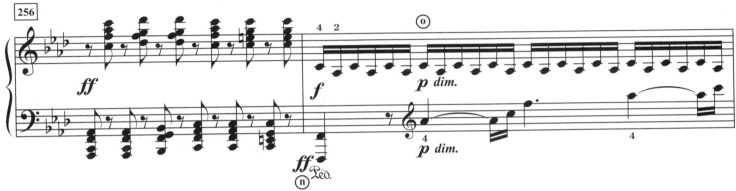

(n) Pedaling in measures 257–262 is from the autograph and first edition, neither of which indicate a release.

(o) Arrau, Casella, and Taylor recommend crossing the LH over the RH. Martienssen, Schenker, and Tovey suggest playing the LH under the RH. Playing the LH under the RH is more awkward initially, but uncrossing the hands is easier on beat 4 of measure 259. Bülow, Casella, and Taylor offer the following facilitation:

This editor, however, finds the facilitation as hard as the original uncrossing.

Andante con moto

225

228

(a) The autograph and the first edition differ with regard to the arpeggiation in measures 101 and 102. The main text follows the autograph: an arpeggio symbol running through both staves in measure 101 and only for the LH in measure 102. The word *arpeggio* attends the LH in measure 102. The word *secco* for the RH, in this case, is believed to be a direction to play the RH notes together as a chord. The first edition omits the term *secco* in measure 102 and indicates individual arpeggio symbols for both the RH and the LH in both measures. Of the referenced editors, only d'Albert, Bülow, Krebs, and Köhler follow the first edition. The other editors print the autograph version, and Casella, Schnabel, Taylor, Tovey, and Wallner point to the difference in notes. This editor prefers the version in the autograph.

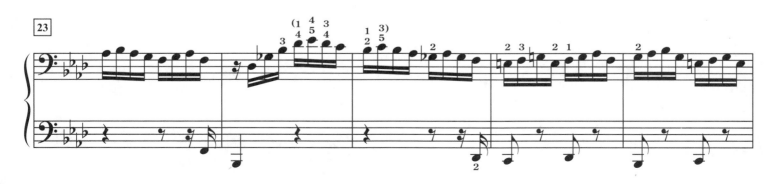

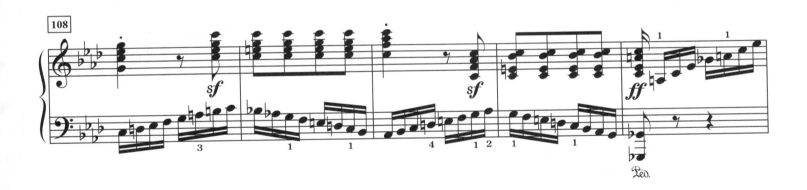

(a) The autograph shows the quarter note chords in measures 104, 106, 108, 110, 296, and 298 with staccato marks. These do not appear in the first edition. Only Hauschild, Schenker, Taylor, Wallner, and this editor follow the autograph. The other referenced editors do not include the staccato marks, and d'Albert, Bülow, Casella, and Schenker even add tenuto marks to these chords.

(b) Both the autograph and the first edition are missing the natural sign before the last sixteenth note in the LH of measures 105 and 107. No one seems to doubt that these are omissions. The accidentals before the LH D's in measures 109 and 111 are in dispute, on the other hand. The autograph shows naturals before both D's, the first edition shows flats. Only Arrau, Schenker, Taylor, Wallner, and this editor follow the autograph. The remaining referenced editors follow the first edition.

234

ⓒ Beethoven wrote in the autograph *la seconda parte due volte* in addition to the repeat sign, an indication of how important this repeat was to the composer.

236

(d) The pedaling in measures 176–211 is the same in the autograph and the first edition. Pedal releases are clear and precise: at the ends of measures 178 and 182, beat 2 of measures 187, 189, and 191. Re-pedaling occurs at the *sempre Ped.* indication at measure 192, releasing at measure 204, re-pedaling at measure 206, and releasing at the last bass sixteenth note of measure 211. Following Beethoven's scheme of alternating sonority and silence creates a wonderful atmosphere of suspense.

(e) The autograph shows the LH in measure 211 with a tie between the beat 1 quarter note and subsequent dotted eighth note. The tie is missing in the first edition. D'Albert, Bülow, Köhler, Krebs, Martienssen, and Schnabel follow the first edition and show no tie. Tovey shows none in the text but indicates in a note that it is in the autograph. Casella, Hauschild, Schenker, Taylor, and Wallner point to the discrepancy in notes but opt for the autograph, thus showing the tie. This editor prefers using the tie, for it conforms to the LH motive established in measures 21–22, 23–24, etc.

(f) The autograph shows *rinforzando* in measure 226; the first edition *ritardando*. The first edition is deemed to be in error by all of the referenced editors except d'Albert, Bülow, Krebs, and Köhler.

(g) Playing all the notes in the LH repeated chords in measures 309, 311, and 313–315 may not be possible for small hands. Leaving out the uppermost C preserves the thickness of the texture, but weakens the sound of the dominant. Leaving out the middle G relieves the hand somewhat and preserves the strength of the dominant octave, but compromises the gruffness of the chord texture. The performer who cannot manage the entire chord will simply have to choose.

(h) The *più f* in measure 312 appears in the autograph, but not the first edition.

ⓘ The LH *sf* markings in measures 352, 354, 356, and 358 are in the autograph, but not the first edition. Arrau, Hauschild, Schenker, Taylor, and this editor include them. The other referenced editors do not.

ⓙ In measure 362, the autograph shows A-flats in the bass on the first and third eighth notes. The first edition shows F's. In the autograph, Beethoven wrote but scratched out another ending to the sonata. The rejected ending shows F's in the analogous measure. Only Wallner and Taylor comment on this, the rest of the referenced editors showing the F's of the first edition without comment. Wallner points to the scratched out measure and suggests that the composer mistakenly wrote A-flats for F's. Only Taylor argues for the legitimacy of the A-flats, believing their use to be a deliberate recall of the opening notes of the sonata.

About the
Op. 78

The Op. 78 was probably completed by July, 1809, for it is listed in a note from the composer to a messenger as one of the works he was dispatching, undoubtedly to Breitkopf & Härtel (although Beethoven mistakenly refers to the key of the work as F-sharp minor). The work was published by Breitkopf & Härtel in November of 1810. The autograph is extant.

Op. 78 title page from the first edition, reproduced by kind permission from the copy in the Austrian National Library, Hoboken Collection, S. H. Beethoven 333

The sonata is dedicated to the Countess (Maria) Therese Brunsvik. She, her sisters Josephine and Charlotte (1782–1843), as well as her brother Franz, to whom the Op. 57 is dedicated, enjoyed a close relationship with Beethoven. Therese never married, and after the death of Josephine dedicated herself to charitable works involving young children. In a letter dating from January 1811, the composer thanks Therese for a portrait of herself she had sent, probably painted by the younger Johann Baptist Lampi (1775–1837). The picture was still in the composer's home at the time of his death. Therese's diaries, published in 1938, reveal many of the details of the closeness between Beethoven and the Brunsvik family (see also this volume's introduction to the Op. 57). Alexander Wheelock Thayer (1817–1897), considered to be Beethoven's first scholarly biographer, tried to make a case for Therese as the subject of Beethoven's famous love letter to the "Immortal Beloved." Subsequent scholars have found Thayer's reasoning faulty in this regard.

Sonata No. 24 in F-sharp Major, Op. 78

Autograph/facsimile:	survived
Sketches/loose pages:	none
First edition:	Breitkopf & Härtel: Leipzig, 1810

The first movement of the Op. 78 opens with a four-measure slow (*Adagio cantabile*) introduction that sets the stage for the lyricism of the sonata-allegro movement, marked *Allegro, ma non troppo*, but is not directly related thematically to what follows. The movement itself is compact, both sections marked to be repeated. The first theme area culminates in a climactic cadence in the dominant (upbeat to measure 5 through the downbeat of 28). A short second theme area (upbeat to measure 29–39) leads to endings for repeating the exposition or moving on. The first theme is briefly developed and fragmented in the development (upbeat to measure 41–58). The recapitulation is regular (upbeat to measure 59–108), its final sixteenth-note figuration being extended to form a short coda in which the opening theme is once again stated.

The pattern of the *Allegro vivace* second movement is **A B A B A** coda. The movement is filled with quick dynamic changes and surprising harmonic shifts, making it one of the composers most jovial. The opening **A** section consists of two ideas: a short rhythmic motive that opens with an augmented sixth harmony (measures 1–11) and a rapid sixteenth-note couplet pattern over a legato bass line (measure 12 through the downbeat of 22). The respective appearances of **A** are in the keys of F-sharp major (measure 1 through the downbeat of 22), B major (measure 89 through the downbeat of 110), and F-sharp major (measures 150–161). Extended transitions before the return of each **A** section should be noted. The two **B** sections (measure 57 through the downbeat of 74 and measure 116 through the downbeat of 133) make use of the couplets introduced in **A**, but seem not to be able to decide whether the major or minor mode will dominate. Finally, the minor wins out and the two sections settle in D-sharp and F-sharp minor respectively. The final statement of **A** is extended to form a short coda (measures 161–183).

Beethoven's autographs of Sonata No. 24 in F-sharp Major, *Op. 78, second movement, measures 1–21*

Dedicated to the Countess (Maria) Therese Brunsvik

Sonata No. 24 in F-sharp Major

Ludwig van Beethoven (1770–1827)
Op. 78

(a) An unhurried turn is recommended here. D'Albert,
Bülow, Casella, and Schnabel recommend the following:

(b) Bülow and Casella recommend holding the RH A-sharp through to the end of the measure, an idea justifiably criticized by
Schnabel, Tovey, and Taylor. Neither the autograph nor the first edition support such a change, and the open fifth at the end
of the measure prepares the way for the A-sharp on the upbeat of the *Allegro, ma non troppo*.

(c) D'Albert and Bülow erroneously indicate the time signature ₵ rather than C.

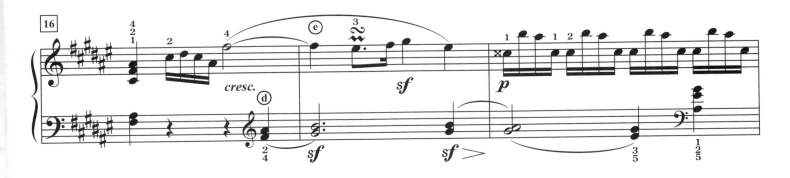

(d) The LH of beat 4 of measure 16 and the first part of
measure 17 reads in both the autograph and the first edition as follows:

Most editors assume this version to be erroneous and match these measures to their counterparts in the recapitulation
(measures 77–78). Hauschild and Wallner acknowledge the discrepancy. Schnabel ponders it in a note, concluding that the
early sources might be right, but allowing the alteration in the main body of the text. Only Taylor argues for the correctness
of the early sources, including their version in the main body of the text and pointing to the fact that Beethoven also uses different
placements of the *sf* markings in the exposition and recapitulation, the former being placed on the downbeat of measure 17 and the
latter on the upbeat to measure 78.

(e) See footnote (b) to the first movement of Op. 54 (page 186) for C.P.E. Bach's realization of this "trilled turn." At the tempo of
this movement, that realization will have the following configuration:

Alternatively, Arrau, Casella, Schenker, Schnabel, and Taylor suggest the following, slightly more difficult realization:

This editor finds the following realizations by d'Albert and Tovey further removed from C.P.E. Bach's example, and more
difficult to execute without sounding rushed:

d'Albert: Tovey:

Bülow and Martienssen suggest a more relaxed version of this concept. However, while pianistically comfortable, these
realizations seem even further removed from early sources:

Bülow: Martienssen:

Apply these comments to measure 78.

(f) The notation in both the autograph and the first edition show measures 25 and 26 with G-naturals in the LH and F-double-sharps in the RH. Similarly, measures 86 and 87 show C-naturals in the LH and B-sharps in the RH. Such unusual combinations trouble some editors, who rewrite the LH enharmonically in these measures.

(g) A variety of opinions exist with regard to the execution of the trills in measures 27 and 88. Arrau, Köhler, and Tovey advise starting on the upper note, presumably on the beat. Bülow and Casella notate an upper accessory grace note before the beat. Hauschild, Schenker, and Wallner show fingering that indicates starting on the main note, and Taylor writes a note that recommends starting on the main note "as was customary at the date of composition." There are no after-notes (nachschlag) in either the autograph or the first edition, but d'Albert, Arrau, Bülow, Köhler, Martienssen, Schenker, Schnabel, and Taylor add them. This editor plays the trill as follows:

measure 27:

(h) Seven of the referenced editors show fingering that suggests starting the trill in measure 43 on the main note. Arrau, Köhler, and Schenker prefer starting on the upper note. Ten of the referenced editors add after-notes (*nachschlag*). This editor plays as follows:

252

(i) Beethoven's fingering shows the LH thumb on the first and third sixteenth notes of beat 4 in measure 104. Casella and Taylor offer similar facilitations of this measure:

Taylor's version:

254

(a) The first two sixteenth notes of measure 47 appear an octave lower than those in measure 16. Because a new page starts at this point in the autograph, eight of the referenced editors deem this an error and render measure 47 like measure 16, with Casella writing a footnote supporting the change. Five of the referenced editors follow the autograph and the first edition, Schnabel arguing in a note for keeping the original, and Taylor and Wallner simply noting the irregularity.

256

ⓑ The pedal markings in this movement (measures 57–59, 61–63, 74–75, 116–118, 120–122, 133–134, 176, and 177) are from both the autograph and the first edition. The points of release are very clearly marked and thus should be precise.

ⓒ The low D-sharp in the LH is not used until measure 71, the note an octave higher being used on the downbeats of measures 67 and 69. Köhler allows the low note for all three measures. Schnabel and Tovey write notes against using the lower pitches. Note that the composer selects another pattern for measures 124–130.

258

(d) The RH fingering in measures 116–117 and 120–121 are from the autograph and the first edition.